DEVELOPING A TEACHING PORTFOLIO

A GUIDE FOR PRESERVICE AND PRACTICING TEACHERS

Second Edition

Ann Adams Bullock
East Carolina University

Parmalee P. Hawk
East Carolina University

PEARSON

Merrill
Prentice Hall

Upper Saddle River, New Jersey
Columbus, Ohio

Library of Congress Cataloging-in-Publication Data

Adams-Bullock, Ann.
  Developing a teaching portfolio: a guide for preservice and practicing teachers/Ann Adams Bulloc.—Two ed.
    p. cm.
  Includes bibliographical references and index.
  ISBN 0-13-113213-X
    1. Portfolios in education—United States. 2. Teachers—Rating of—United States.
  3. Teachers—Training of—United States. I. Hawk, Parmalee P. II. Title.

  LB1728.A32 2004
  371.14′4—dc22

                                                    2004012618

Vice President and Executive Publisher: Jeffery W. Johnston
Executive Editor: Debra A. Stollenwerk
Editorial Assistant: Mary Morrill
Production Editor: Kris Roach
Production Coordination: The GTS Companies/York, PA Campus
Design Coordinator: Diane C. Lorenzo
Cover Designer: Bryan Huber
Cover image: Getty One
Photo Coordinator: Kathy Kirtland
Production Manager: Susan Hannahs
Director of Marketing: Ann Castel Davis
Marketing Manager: Darcy Betts Prybella
Marketing Coordinator: Tyra Poole

Photo Credits: All photos by Ann Adams Bullock

This book was set in Palatino by The GTS Companies/York, PA Campus. It was printed and bound by Phoenix Color Book Group. The cover was printed by Phoenix Color Corp.

Pearson Prentice Hall™ is a trademark of Pearson Education, Inc.
Pearson® is a registered trademark of Pearson plc
Prentice Hall® is a registered trademark of Pearson Education, Inc.
Merrill® is a registered trademark of Pearson Education, Inc.

Pearson Education Ltd.
Pearson Education Singapore Pte. Ltd.
Pearson Education Canada, Ltd.
Pearson Education—Japan

Pearson Education Australia Pty. Limited
Pearson Education North Asia Ltd.
Pearson Educación de Mexico, S.A. de C.V.
Pearson Education Malaysia Pte. Ltd.

10 9 8 7 6 5 4 3 2 1
ISBN: 0-13-113213-X

PREFACE

oday, many teachers think they have become scapegoats for all the problems facing education. Their feelings are a result of the wave of reform initiatives in the past 25 years that have focused on the classroom teacher. This focus is supported by research that reports that the most salient element for a child's academic achievement is the quality of his or her classroom teacher. How to determine that quality has evolved through two decades of accountability efforts. The passage of the No Child Left Behind legislation places increased emphasis on how to determine the "quality" of teachers. How the nation will define quality is yet to be clearly revealed, but the momentum for using portfolios continues to grow. *Developing a Teaching Portfolio: A Guide for Preservice and Practicing Teachers* speaks to this form of assessment and concentrates on how a teacher can use the portfolio process to demonstrate his or her competence as a professional.

Developing a Teaching Portfolio is a book that can be used in teacher preparation programs, as staff development for practicing teachers to teach the portfolio development process, or for individuals interested in the portfolio process. It focuses on using portfolios throughout one's professional career. Before progressing through each chapter, let's consider what is new to this edition:

1. At the end of a section or chapter are activities for preservice or inservice teachers to complete. These will give teachers the opportunity to practice the new concept or skill in a safe, nonpunitive environment.
2. There are more examples of portfolios, reflections, analyses, rubrics, and statewide assessment systems.

3. Former chapters 6 and 7 have been combined into one chapter (Chapter 6) about portfolios for licensure, whether the teacher is a beginner or a veteran.
4. The chapter on digital portfolios has been expanded with activities that will guide even the most inexperienced user of technology.
5. Dependable Web sites have been added so that students and teachers can search on their own for additional information about portfolios and their use.
6. Updated appendixes provide additional information and standards of interest to the consumer.

Please remember, Chapters 1 through 3 are required reading regardless of the teacher's career stage. Chapter 1 provides a brief overview of the accountability and teacher assessment movements. Chapter 2 describes a portfolio and the different types of portfolios that one can develop. Because reflections are the very heart of the portfolio process, Chapter 3 is devoted to the "what, why, when, and how" of writing a reflection. This opening section of the book also addresses the legal issues involved with portfolios and the assessment and scoring of them.

Chapters 4 through 7 are dedicated to what portfolios should include and how teachers go about developing a portfolio at different stages of their careers. Chapters 4 and 5 center on the development of portfolios during the years that teachers are novices. Chapter 4's focus is on preservice teachers, and Chapter 5 spotlights using the portfolio to obtain employment. Chapter 6 concentrates on preparing a portfolio for continuing licensure and license renewal. Chapter 7 hones in on the master teacher who is seeking national board certification.

Chapter 8 provides instruction on the use of digital portfolios at any stage of one's career. This chapter presents the pros and cons of developing an electronic portfolio and makes suggestions concerning the hardware and software one would use. Our colleague Dr. Ivan Wallace contributed his expertise to this chapter.

Acknowledgments

In writing this book, we have been influenced by our own experiences as teachers and researchers. In addition, much of our knowledge about portfolios and their development has come from working with over 300 teachers in elementary grades, middle grades, and secondary schools. They have provided us with all the examples in this book (we did not make up the examples) and helped us gather data on portfolio "trials, tribulations, and benefits." Therefore, we gratefully acknowledge the many teachers who permitted us to learn from them and who willingly provided us with reflections, pieces of evidence, and portfolio products. Without them this book would not exist.

A special thanks to Carolyn Smith, Nicole Byrd-Phelps, Kelly Cave, Russell Vernon, and the 1997–2003 middle grades majors at East Carolina University.

Also, special thanks to Art Bouthillier for the use of his cartoon "The First Portfolio," and to Scott Thomson for his original cartoons created specifically for this text. To Peggy Hopkins, Mamie Blevins, Kermit Buckner, and Eddie Ingram, we express our appreciation for all the intensive work they have done on the North Carolina Performance-Based Product Handbook, which is in Appendix B. Also in Appendix B are portions of the State of Connecticut's portfolio, which can be found at www.state.ct.us/ sde/dtl/t-a/index.htm.

Many thanks to Dr. Ivan Wallace, chair of business, career, and technical education at East Carolina University, for sharing his expertise related to digital portfolios. Our "Thank Heaven Award" goes to Sherry Tripp, who made a valiant effort to keep us on track during the first- and second-edition manuscripts. We also want to thank the reviewers for their insightful comments. They are Elaine Chakonas, Northern Illinois University; Betty Epanchin, University of South Florida; Tom Gregory, Indiana University, Bloomington; Barbara Kacer, Western Kentucky University; Rebekah Kelleher, Wingate University; and Ling Marcelene, Western Oregon State College.

Finally, the authors would like to thank our editor, Debbie Stollenwerk, at Merrill/Prentice Hall and the editors and staff at the GTS Companies, whose positive comments and work ethic contributed to a successful second edition.

INTRODUCTION

Each day a teacher makes over 3,000 decisions in the classroom. At the end of each day, in each teacher's classroom, children have achieved in many ways. Current evaluation tools don't allow teachers to show their "real" experiences and successes as a teacher. Portfolios provide an avenue for you, as an educator, to show the depth and breadth of your profession. If this is your first time creating a portfolio, or if you have used one for a purpose other than teacher evaluation, this book will provide both the foundation and the specifics to be successful in this endeavor. You will find this book easy to read and follow. Information, tips, and examples are provided for teachers at all stages—from those in teacher education programs to those who are interested in national board certification. This book is divided into two parts: Chapters 1 through 3 give the background and provide the foundational knowledge of portfolio development; Chapters 4 through Chapter 8 provide specifics and suggestions for teachers and other educators. You should read all of Part I and those chapters in Part II that match your needs as a portfolio developer or facilitator.

Chapter 1 provides a chronological story of the milestones of teacher evaluation and changes in the educational field. It gives background information on the ways portfolios are used by teachers at different stages of their careers and the reasons why. This chapter is essential to understand the context for portfolio development. Chapter 2 is crucial because it defines the types of portfolios and components of each. It outlines process, product, and showcase portfolios and the rationale for each. The depth and diversity of portfolio development is portrayed in this chapter.

The ability to reflect is the cornerstone of portfolio development. Chapter 3 examines the specifics on writing reflections well and ends with examples and sample prompts. In our first edition, this chapter was deemed the most important and the most useful in the entire book. The detailed steps for reflective writing provide instructions and processes for the beginning reflective practitioner. Chapters 1, 2, and 3 are the foundation of this book. You will find the information in these chapters useful in defining the purpose of portfolio development, and in learning the skills necessary to be a successful developer.

Part II is much like a buffet at a restaurant. Depending on individual likes and wants, different chapters will be chosen by different readers. Chapter 4 is for those beginning to teach. Candidates in teacher education programs will find specific examples and tips to create a portfolio when it is a requirement for their program. If you are seeking a job, Chapter 5 gives you tips for compiling a portfolio. Chapter 6 is for the practicing teacher, whether he or she is beginning or has many years of experience. It includes examples of teacher licensure requirements and of portfolios used as a teacher evaluation tool. Many systems allow teachers to create a portfolio rather than be observed. Experienced teachers will want to read Chapter 7, which focuses on national board certification. This capstone experience for experienced teachers will provide outstanding professional development for those who have taught for 5, 10, or 25 years. Chapter 7 outlines national board processes and standards, and offers sample activities. In Chapter 8, digital portfolios are discussed. Dr. Ivan Wallace gives excellent advice and examples of this varied format for creating portfolios at any stage of one's career. Finally, the appendixes provide additional examples and information for all readers.

It is our intent for this book to give teachers at all stages of careers the tools and resources necessary to become reflective practitioners who take charge of their destiny as professionals. The portfolio allows teachers to show their depth and breadth as educators. It provides an opportunity for diverse documentation of the teacher's impact on students. Congratulations on the decision to create a living document of your experiences—the portfolio.

BRIEF CONTENTS

CONTENTS

ix

PART II Applications of Portfolio Development   53

FOUNDATIONS FOR PORTFOLIO DEVELOPMENT

This book is presented in two parts. The first part, Chapters 1 through 3, is intended for all readers. These chapters present background information and specific details on portfolio development for all teachers and provide the foundation for the second part of the book. Chapter 1 explores the metamorphosis of portfolio development. Chapter 2 gives specific information on how to develop a portfolio. Chapter 3 addresses reflection, the critical component of portfolio development. After reading these three chapters, readers will have the background and information needed to move to the second part of this book.

Please note: Chapters 1 through 3 are necessary for all readers.

CHAPTER 1

The Teacher Assessment Movement

Education in the United States is unique when compared to education in other civilized countries, because this country is committed to educating everyone's child. Almost 250 years ago, Thomas Jefferson declared that "if this nation expects to be both ignorant and free, it expects what never was and never will be." Jefferson's words laid the foundation for education in the United States—the education of all children. That daunting task of educating young people for future generations fell to the nation's classroom teachers. With each decade, the teacher's tasks have become more complex and demanding. Today, the challenges are greater than they have ever been, as we see society and the world changing with each passing day.

Periodically, politicians and the public question the quality of education in America. This questioning often emerges as a reaction to the economy and the increasing need for skilled and knowledgeable workers. As a result, numerous national forums, task forces, and commissions are established to study needed reforms. These national committees make recommendations that spawn state task forces, forums, and commissions to implement reform efforts.

THE TEACHER ASSESSMENT MOVEMENT

In the past two decades, there have been numerous calls for the reform of public education, and significant efforts have been made to respond. The watershed event that brought the perceived shortcomings of education into the forefront of the public consciousness was the publication, in 1983, of *A Nation at Risk,* by the National Commission on Excellence in Education. The commission's report was on the failings of the nation's educational system and inadvertently led to harsh criticism of the country's teaching force. A decade later, Terrell Bell, chair of the national commission, stated that the intent of *A Nation at Risk* was to make America aware of the needs of its schools and "was not intended for teachers to receive the blame that was heaped on them" (Bell, 1993, p. 593). However, the reality is that the majority of subsequent reform movements have focused on the need to fill our classrooms with competent teachers.

The Carnegie Forum's 1986 study *A Nation Prepared: Teachers for the 21st Century* recognized that 50 years ago American teachers enjoyed the respect they earned as a result of being among the best educated people in the community. Today, teachers are "victims of their own success" (Bell, 1993, p. 36) because respect for teachers has waned as the education level of the general populace has risen. This "better schooled public" has generated a climate of doubt concerning teachers' competence and their ability to facilitate their students' learning.

During the 1990s, the National Commission on Teaching and America's Future studied the educational scene in *What Matters Most: Teaching for Americas Future* (1996). Its 2-year study concluded that the reform of elementary and secondary education depended primarily on restructuring the teaching profession. The commission's findings reported that "a caring, competent, and qualified teacher is the most important ingredient in education reform."

In the spring of 2002, Congress passed the most sweeping federal education legislation enacted since Title I was funded in the 1960s. For the first time, the federal government established accountability standards, with serious consequences for public schools not meeting the new student achievement levels. The No Child Left Behind (NCLB) legislation has called for "highly qualified teachers" in every classroom, for every student. Schools and teachers will be held accountable for all of their students' academic achievement.

Richard Dollase, in *Voices of Beginning Teachers: Visions and Realities,* cites a 1989 report of the Association of American Colleges that defines what constitutes a high-quality teacher: "a broadly educated individual who has command of both the subjects to be taught and of the ways which they can be taught effectively to the range of students he or she will be teaching" (p. 1). The quandary is how a nation assures its citizens that this type of teacher resides in all its classrooms with all its children. One way the

NCLB suggests is to hold teachers accountable for their teaching and associated duties.

ACCOUNTABILITY

The accountability movement has become a part of the educational landscape in the latter part of the 20th century. Over the past 30 years, states have assumed increasing responsibility for schools as the federal government has disbursed education funds to states and, more recently, pushed for deficit reductions. As a result, education has had increased visibility in state budgets and increased attention from legislators. This attention becomes greater as elected state officials explain to their constituencies what kind of education the state money is buying. To provide the public with data on how effectively the state money is being spent, a push to hold schools accountable for their students' performance has become prevalent (Elmore, 1997).

In the 1970s, the teacher empowerment movement began to spread across the nation. Teacher organizations were becoming more powerful as they recognized education budget cutbacks and salary increases lagging behind the cost of living. They supported more involvement of teachers in the development of local curricula and in the management of local schools. Organizations such as the National Education Association (NEA) began to lobby for autonomous professional standards boards that would be involved in program approval processes for teacher education programs, shared governance of these programs, and the assessment of classroom teachers. By 2002, 16 states had established professional standards boards with teachers as the majority of members on each (U.S. Department of Education, 2002).

With growing input and representation in the decision-making process, teachers increasingly are being held accountable for their students' performance. Nearly all states have increased their testing agendas and formulated statewide standards for student performance. Should teachers be held accountable for student learning? Wang, Haertel, and Walberg (1990), for example, contend that the extent of student learning in a given year is influenced by many factors that lie beyond the teacher's control. Still, many states consider student performance the center of accountability. It has resulted in mandates for "outcomes assessment" to better measure what students are learning (Kruckeberg, 1995).

The pressures of standards and assessments are increasingly present, with the classroom teacher being held accountable for student learning. In fact, in the summer of 2003, Public Agenda, a nonpartisan research group, reported that many teachers think they are the scapegoats for all the learning problems of children. Those surveyed (1,345 teachers) also reported that they like their jobs but are frustrated by the ever-changing standards that teachers must meet.

EVOLUTION OF TEACHER ASSESSMENT

Over the first half of this century, teaching was a profession for women and college-educated minorities who possessed few other options for employment. When young White men did teach, it was usually to start them on their "ladder of success" to an administrative position or a different profession altogether. Since the early 1960s, the social demographics have changed. The two-income family has become the rule rather than the exception, and women and minorities have increased opportunities in other fields. These social changes have had a twofold effect on the number of teachers entering classrooms, particularly in the 1970s. First, the turnover rate for female teachers decreased, which led to fewer job openings for new teacher education graduates. Second, as the opportunities in society increased for women and minorities, these groups prepared for positions with better financial rewards, thus depleting the steady supply of new teachers. When large numbers of teachers reached retirement age, beginning in the mid-1980s, emergency and alternative credentialing of individuals without education degrees became prevalent. National reports coupled with the social factors of the last 30 years have been an impetus for teacher assessment (Taskforce on Teaching as a Profession, 1986).

In the 1970s, competency-based teacher preparation programs emerged. Competencies are knowledge, skills, and behaviors that are stated in advance, can be demonstrated, and are possible to assess. The competency-based movement bore a resemblance to the behavioral objectives of the 1960s. It also brought major teacher testing initiatives during that decade. These were tests with multiple-choice questions assessing basic literacy, professional knowledge, and subject matter knowledge (Haertel, 1991). The National Teacher's Exam (NTE) was the most widely used of these tests. These tests were later seen to fall short of measuring many important teaching skills, and in the 1980s there was a proliferation of classroom observation instruments developed to assess teachers' performances. These observation instruments were anchored to teaching effectiveness research, which showed empirical correlations of teaching practices to student achievement. By the early 1980s, Florida, Georgia, South Carolina, and North Carolina had performance appraisal instruments in place to assess teachers' teaching skills. Many other states soon followed. Though observer evaluations are generally deemed helpful tools, they have inadequacies in assessing some important aspects of teaching (i.e., student learning, student assessment, planning, and reflection on teaching). In addition, observations by someone else, usually a principal, central office person, or peer, place the responsibility for providing data regarding the teacher's performance into other hands. It is not the teacher, the primary stakeholder, who bears the burden of presenting data; it is whoever performed the observation.

Teaching has always been viewed as a complex set of behaviors and attitudes that converge in the classroom to create the type of interaction that is conducive to student learning. Teaching is part science and part art, and the research debate on the merits of personal attributes versus technical approaches has raged for several decades (Haertel, 1991). However, most researchers agree that establishing the purpose of evaluation is a critical initial step in the development of a teacher evaluation process or instrument. The purpose of the observation instruments mentioned earlier was to see if teachers demonstrated a given set of behaviors. The 1986 Carnegie Report helped advance this purpose when it recommended new performance-based assessment instruments using standards.

Before progressing into a discussion of new assessment standards, the word *standard* must be clarified. In their monograph *A Brief History of Standards in Teacher Education*, Edelfelt and Raths (1998) note that educators have been concerned about standards for more than a century. Pearson (1994) defines *standard* as "a definite level of degree of quality that is proper or adequate for a specific purpose; something that is established by authority, custom, or general consent as a model or example to be followed." He includes *criterion, gauge, yardstick*, and *test* as alternate words. Today, *standard* is used as a synonym for *criterion* (Edelfelt & Raths, p. 3).

In the 1986 Carnegie Report, educational reform was charted in the direction of new assessment instruments and standards with the following suggestions:

- Admission to teacher education programs should be contingent on applicants' mastery of basic skills and the knowledge expected of all college graduates.
- States and others should offer incentives for students of exceptional academic ability, and to minority candidates who qualify to attend graduate teacher-education programs.
- A national board for professional teaching standards should be created to establish standards for high levels of professional teaching competencies and to issue certificates to people meeting those standards.
- State and local policy should encourage institutions of higher education and other providers to develop programs of continuing education to keep teachers abreast of the field and to prepare them for meeting the National Board standards.

The National Board for Professional Teaching Standards (NBPTS), proposed by the Carnegie Forum, was established in 1987 and has developed, and continues to develop, assessment instruments for the national certification of teachers. The NBPTS assessments provide a more complex and richer means of verifying teacher competence using much of the process envisioned by Lee Shulman (1987), who wrote:

> I no longer think of assessment of teachers as an activity involving a single test or even a battery of tests. I envision a process that unfolds and extends over time, in which written tests of knowledge, systematic documentation or accomplishments, formal attestations by colleagues and supervisors and analyses of performance in assessment centers and in the workplace are combined and integrated in a variety of ways to achieve a representation of a candidate's pedagogical capacities.

With the impetus of the Carnegie Forum's 1986 statement that "[teachers] must demonstrate that they have a command of the needed knowledge and ability to apply it," and Shulman's leadership, the NBPTS assessment emerged. A teacher seeking national certification prepares a portfolio, based on specific standards, and completes written assessments to measure his or her content knowledge.

NATIONAL BOARD FOR PROFESSIONAL TEACHING STANDARDS

The National Board for Professional Teaching Standards had begun establishing a "professional model" as opposed to "a bureaucratic model" for teacher assessment. Its process is to determine what knowledge bases and practices teachers must know and be able to do. This professional model is undergirded by the educational beliefs that (a) individuals learn more when they are responsible for their own learning and development and (b) individuals perform at a high level of competence when high expectations and outcomes are clearly stated. This professional model enables teachers to demonstrate and document their competence rather than depend on someone else to document it. The NBPTS standards follow and will be discussed in greater depth in Chapter 7:

1. Teachers are committed to students and their learning.
2. Teachers know the subjects they teach and how to teach those subjects to students.
3. Teachers are responsible for managing and monitoring student learning.
4. Teachers think systematically about their practice and learn from experience.
5. Teachers are members of a learning community.

These standards are designed for experienced competent teachers who will receive a national certification if they successfully meet the established assessment criteria.

The NBPTS process gives experienced teachers the opportunity to take responsibility for demonstrating the depth of their knowledge and skills. To use this professional model with teachers early in their careers, new assessment procedures needed to be put in place. With new state initiatives, the responsibilities for all teachers are broadening. Beginning teachers, as well as experienced ones, must perform instructional planning for both their classrooms and their schools, participate in the governance of the school, and participate in expanding their knowledge and understanding of students. All these issues point to more encompassing means of assessing new teachers' performance. One of the most promising efforts to this end has been the development of assessment standards by the Interstate New Teacher Assessment and Support Consortium (INTASC).

INTASC STANDARDS

INTASC standards were developed under the auspices of the Council of Chief State Officers, a consortium of 37 states dedicated to the basic idea that content knowledge is wedded to pedagogical understanding, and if students are to learn, teachers must master these two areas. The INTASC approach requires beginning teachers to demonstrate entry-level competencies of teaching through the development of a portfolio. The INTASC standards contain two important attributes:

1. They are performance-based assessments where teachers describe what they know and are able to do once they have entered the profession.
2. They are linked to current views of what students should know and be able to do in order to meet K–12 standards for learning.

INTASC standards are not rigid in design. They recognize that teachers work in a wide variety of circumstances with populations that are diverse in ethnicity, home language, socioeconomic status, and gender (Ambach, 1996; Shapiro, 1995).

The states and programs that have adopted the INTASC standards have chosen to follow the NBPTS assessment format—the portfolio. Connecticut and North Carolina are two states that have adopted the INTASC standards and have designed licensure procedures using portfolios. The INTASC standards follow and will be discussed further in Chapters 2 and 5:

1. The teacher understands the central concepts, tools of inquiry, and structures of the discipline he or she teaches and can create learning experiences that make these aspects of subject matter meaningful to students.
2. The teacher understands how children learn and develop, and can provide learning opportunities that support a child's intellectual, social, and personal development.
3. The teacher understands how students differ in their approaches to learning and creates instructional opportunities that are adapted to diverse learners.
4. The teacher understands and uses a variety of instructional strategies to encourage student development of critical thinking, problem solving, and performance skills.
5. The teacher uses an understanding of individual and group motivation and behavior to create a learning environment that encourages positive social interaction, active engagement in learning, and self-motivation.
6. The teacher uses knowledge of effective verbal, nonverbal, and media communication techniques to foster active inquiry, collaboration, and supportive interaction in the classroom.
7. The teacher plans instruction based upon knowledge of the subject matter, students, community, and curriculum goals.
8. The teacher understands and uses formal and informal assessment strategies to evaluate and ensure the continuous intellectual, social, and physical development of the learner.

9. The teacher is a reflective practitioner who continually evaluates the effects of his or her choices and actions on others (students, parents, and other professionals in the learning community) and who actively seeks out opportunities to grow professionally.
10. The teacher fosters relationships with school colleagues, parents, and agencies in the larger community to support students' learning and well-being.

The NBPTS and INTASC standards are affecting not only the ways teachers are assessed, but also the ways teachers are educated. This is evidenced by their incorporation into the National Council for the Accreditation of Teacher Education's (NCATE) accreditation process for teacher preparation programs. New NCATE standards are being developed with increased focus on the performance of the college's or university's education graduates:

> The emphasis on performance has been spurred by a realization among policymakers that changes in curriculum and courses have not significantly increased student achievement. The number one factor in enhancing student learning is the capability of the teacher. How to determine quality and knowledge are central questions as NCATE develops its performance-based accreditation system. (Wise, 1998, p. 1)

These new NCATE standards not only measure a teacher preparation program through its new graduates' performance but also through their performance as they move from beginning teachers to continuing teachers. This accountability for colleges and universities is providing the impetus for many to incorporate a performance product, such as a portfolio, into their teacher preparation programs.

The No Child Left Behind (NCLB) legislation requires the testing of teachers to demonstrate their content knowledge. However, testing does not help teachers demonstrate their ability to motivate and facilitate students to learn, nor does it enable them to reflect on their teaching successes or failures. For this reason, portfolios are becoming a useful partner to teacher testing.

CLOSING THOUGHTS

The last decade and a half has spawned numerous national reports on the state of education in America. These have generated new assessment instruments using standards that urge educators to be more accountable. The instruments most prominently used to assess the performance of teachers have evolved from paper-and-pencil testing to classroom observations to portfolio development.

Portfolios are a complex assessment process, more so than classroom observations. They provide two distinct advantages over testing and classroom observations. First, portfolios build a professional model of assessment, not a bureaucratic model. They enable the teacher to be more "in charge" of his or her evaluation. Second, though teachers find the portfolios time-consuming to compile, they report experiencing considerable professional growth from the process (Hawk, 1996).

The portfolio type of performance-based product responds to the higher standards called for in *A Nation Prepared* and *What Matters Most: Teaching for America's Future*. Although the NCLB legislation appears to be favoring testing to establish teachers' qualifications, at least two major meta-analyses of education research are in progress and will report that knowing content is important, but knowing how to teach that content is the key to student achievement (Rice, 2003). Portfolios provide teachers with the opportunity to document subject-specific pedagogy and the ways in which their students have achieved.

WEB SITES

Center for Teaching Quality
www.teachingquality.org

Education Commission of the States
www.ecs.org

Education News
www.educationnews.org

Education Week
www.edweek.org

REFERENCES

Ambach, G. (1996). Standards for teachers: Potential for improving practice. *Phi Delta Kappan, 78*(3), 207–210.

Bell, T. (1993). Reflections on one decade after *A nation at risk. Phi Delta Kappan, 74*(4), 592–597.

Dollase, R. (1992). *Voices of beginning teachers: Visions and realities.* New York: Teachers College Press.

Edelfelt, R. A., & Raths, J. D. (1998). *A brief history of standards in teacher education.* Washington, DC: Association of Teacher Educators.

Elmore, R. F. (1997). Accountability in local school districts: Learning to do the right things. *Advances in Educational Administration, 5,* 59–82.

Haertel, E. (1991). New forms of teacher assessment. *Review of Research in Education, 17,* 3–30.

Hawk, P. P. (1996). *Performance-based assessment.* Raleigh, NC: North Carolina Department of Public Instruction.

Interstate New Teacher Assessment and Support Consortium. (1992). *Model standards for beginning teacher licensing and development: A resource for state dialog*. Washington, DC: Council of Chief State School Officers.

Johnson, J., & Duffen, A. (2003). *Where we are now*. Reston, VA: Public Agenda.

Kruckeberg, D. (1995, August). *Public relations education and outcomes assessment: An immediate challenge for educators*. Paper presented at the 78th annual meeting of the Association for Education in Journalism and Mass Media, Washington, DC.

National Commission on Teaching America's Future. (1996). *What matters most: Teaching for America's future*. Retrieved April 7, 2004, from http://www. zuni.k12.nm.us/ Ias/21TE/NWREL/what.htm

Paulson, F., Paulson, P., & Meyer, L. (1991). What makes a portfolio a portfolio? *Educational Leadership, 48*(5), 60–63.

Pearson, P. D. (1994). Standards and teacher education: A policy perception. In M. E. Diez, V. Richardson, & P. Pearson (Eds.), *Setting standards and educating teachers* (pp. 37–67). Washington, DC: American Association of Colleges of Teacher Education.

Rice, J. K. (2003). *Teacher quality: Understanding the effectiveness of teaching attributes*. Retrieved April 7, 2004, from http://www.epinet.org

Shapiro, B. (1995). National standards for teachers. *Streamline Seminars, 13*(4).

Shulman, L. S. (1987). Those who understand: Knowledge growth in teaching. *Educational Researcher, 15*(2), 4–14.

Taskforce on Teaching as a Profession. (1986). *A nation prepared: Teachers for the 21st century*. New York: Carnegie Forum on Education and the Economy.

U. S. Department of Education. (2002). *Report on state teaching commission*. Washington, DC: Author.

Wang, M. C., Haertel, G. D., & Walberg, H. J. (1990). What influences learning? A content analysis of the literature. *Journal of Educational Research, 84*, 30–43.

Wise, A. E. (1998). NCATE 2000 will emphasize candidate performance. *Quality Teaching, 7*(2), 1–2.

2

Portfolio Development

WHAT IS A PORTFOLIO?

When individuals hear the word *portfolio,* many different images come to mind. Artists think of compiling their best work (e.g., paintings, pottery, portraits, and sculptures) for review, while a portfolio for teachers often contains gathered samples of lesson plans, units of study, and professional documents that reflect the knowledge, skills, and beliefs of the teacher. The artist's portfolio describes each painting, in writing, giving details about artistic design.

Teachers who develop portfolios reflect on each piece of work, highlighting the strengths, weaknesses, and changes he or she would make in his or her teaching. The teacher's portfolio is used for self-evaluation or external review. Both of these images are correct representations of portfolios, because they both have several specific components:

1. They have a specific *purpose.* The artist's portfolio shows his or her artistic abilities, whereas the teacher's portfolio shows his or her knowledge, skills, and abilities.
2. They are developed for a specific *audience.* The artist's audience is a potential employer, and the teacher's is him- or herself or external reviewers.
3. They contain work samples, commonly called *evidence.* Evidence is the "stuff" or "things" that are put into the portfolio. The artist's evidence would be the paintings, pottery, portraits, and sculptures. The teacher's evidence would include lesson plans, units of study, and other professional documents.
4. They have *reflections.* Both the artist and teacher would have written thoughts on the evidence contained in the portfolio.

These examples show that two products can look different but can still be considered portfolios. A portfolio is not merely a manila file filled with assignments or work, nor is it a scrapbook of memorabilia. Campbell, Cignetti, Melenyzer, Nettles, and Wyman (1997) stated that a portfolio is an organized, goal-driven collection of evidence. For educators, portfolios have become more commonplace over the past 5 years. The necessity of national board certification and the adoption of alternative methods of evaluation for teacher candidates and practicing teachers have paved the way. Portfolios have emerged as viable assessment tools for both teacher candidates and practicing teachers. They are a way for teachers to document their professional development, for preservice teachers to measure knowledge, or for teachers to use in the certification process (Adams, 1995; Krause, 1996; Tierney, 1993; Wolf, 1996). There are three different types of portfolios: *progress, product,* and *showcase.* While each type is compiled for a different audience, all have a developer, purpose, specific audience, and *reflection section* (discussed in Chapter 3) on the evidence.

A person chooses whether to develop a process, product, or showcase portfolio based on the purpose for its development. The purpose, otherwise identified as the "why" of portfolio development, is the driving force that determines its organizational design.

Four Components of Portfolios	Three Types of Portfolios
Purpose	Process
Audience	Product
Evidence	Showcase
Reflections	

WHAT IS A PROCESS PORTFOLIO?

A process portfolio shows a person's performance over a period of time. Its purpose isn't to *prove* something, but rather to *improve* something. The goal of this portfolio is to evaluate a teacher's progress in one or more areas over a given period of time. Using writing as an example, the purpose of a process portfolio would be to show how writing is taught in the classroom and the improvement of students' writing over time. The developer would choose evidence that would show how he or she taught writing and the progress of the students over time. Reflections would focus on how writing was taught and the development of the skills and abilities of the students as writers. For example, the teacher might describe a lesson focusing on writing and the successes and areas where the students can improve. Next, the teacher might reflect on what should happen next in the classroom in relation to writing. Evidence would be chosen as the portfolio is developed over the school year. It would represent the successes and weaknesses of the writing program so that a clear portrayal of the teacher's progress is given. Different teachers using writing as a focus could have different evidence, depending on their own development. The process portfolio is commonly used by teachers who want to focus on the development of skills and knowledge.

Process Portfolio

A teacher is creating a process portfolio with the following goal: incorporating cooperative learning into his or her classroom over a school year.

Purpose:
To document the integration of cooperative learning into the classroom

Audience(s):
Self and principal

Types of Evidence:
Staff development certificate and handouts on cooperative learning, lesson plans incorporating cooperative learning over a school year, student work from cooperative groups, copy of grade book showing "grades" from cooperative learning assignments, student surveys about the cooperative learning process, self-evaluation notes from the teacher showing changes made after each cooperative learning lesson, teacher's summary of thoughts about the cooperative learning process

Placed in:
A three-ring notebook

The First Portfolio!

"I kept saying, 'Maybe we should clean off the front of the refrigerator' —but, nooo . . ."

Cartoon by Art Bouthillier. All rights reserved.

EXAMPLE 1

Sample Process Portfolio

Background:
Mr. Clark, a kindergarten teacher, is interested in developing a portfolio to show his process as a teacher, specifically in using developmentally appropriate practices. He wants to show his knowledge, skills, and abilities in this area.

Purpose:
To track progress as a teacher using developmentally appropriate practices

Audience:
Mr. Clark and principal

Developer:
Mr. Clark

Organization:
Portfolio kept in a three-ring notebook

Evidence:
Mr. Clark chooses evidence throughout the year related to using developmentally appropriate practices (DAP). He includes the following evidence:

1. A philosophical statement about the use of DAP in the classroom
2. Lesson plans documenting the use of DAP (several subjects over the year)
3. Unit plans documenting the use of DAP (several over the year)
4. Videotape showing several lessons—one in September, one in December, one in March, and one in May
5. Journal by teacher documenting on a day-to-day basis the implementation of DAP
6. Work from several different students (at different levels) throughout the year
7. Anecdotal records documenting progress of students throughout the year
8. Entries in teacher's journal comparing DAP strategies with those previously used

   Other evidence would be determined by Mr. Clark, depending on the progress of his portfolio.

Reflections:
Mr. Clark wrote reflections about his progress each month. At the end of the year, he wrote a summary and an analysis of the entire process.

Sample Process Portfolio—continued

Assessment:
Each month, Mr. Clark did a self-assessment by writing reflections and his principal assessed his progress at the end of the school year. Based on Mr. Clark's self-assessments and the principal's summative assessment, Mr. Clark determined his next steps in relation to using DAP.

Why Is a Process Portfolio Chosen?
Mr. Clark wants to track his progress over a year. Each teacher may have a different time line for his or her progress.

EXAMPLE 2

Sample Process Portfolio

Background:
Mr. Sauls, a beginning middle school science teacher, is interested in developing a portfolio to show his progress toward using inquiry methods and the acquisition of inquiry skills by students. He teaches sixth grade and has assessed that his students haven't used inquiry skills or processes before. Since he is a beginning teacher, Mr. Sauls has only used inquiry lessons during his student teaching experience.

Purpose:
To track the improvement of students' inquiry skills and processes, and the teacher's ability to facilitate inquiry lessons (two goals)

Audience:
Mr. Sauls and his mentor

Developer:
Mr. Sauls

Organization:
Portfolio kept in an expandable folder (by lesson topic), with one section containing data charts on students in relation to specific skills and processes, along with grade sheets

Evidence:
Mr. Sauls developed his portfolio over a 9-week grading period. As a beginning teacher, he and his mentor (Mrs. Groome) decide that a shorter time period would be better so that he could reflect on his practice holistically and adjust it midway throughout the semester. In addition, this was a goal on his initial growth plan (an evaluation goal-setting tool for beginning teachers).

Sample Process Portfolio—continued

He included the following evidence:

1. A list of intended goals and objectives for the 9-week period related to inquiry skills and processes (five inquiry lessons over 9 weeks)
2. A journal in which he wrote his reflections after each inquiry lesson
3. A data chart marked with x's for each child to denote if the inquiry process and skills were observed by the teacher or assessed through written work
4. Sample work from a variety of students (bad and good work) for each of the five lessons
5. An observation from the mentor for two of the inquiry lessons
6. Students' self-evaluation form (a guided question sheet) that was used after three of the inquiry lessons
7. Students' grades on inquiry lesson
8. Assistant principal evaluation of one inquiry lesson (observation)

Reflections:
Mr. Sauls wrote journal reflections about his progress and his students' progress and knowledge after each inquiry lesson.

Assessment:
At the end of the 9-week period he met with his mentor, and they reviewed all of the materials to decide what type of progress was made in the area of inquiry lessons.

Why Was a Process Portfolio Chosen?
Mr. Sauls wanted some data on his effectiveness as a beginning teacher. He wanted to improve his instruction and the skills of his students. He knew there would be improvements and adjustments to be made, and this portfolio type allows for them. In addition, his mentor helped decide on this type of portfolio because it was "less threatening" and allowed for collaboration.

Other Examples of Process Portfolio Goals

1. Mrs. Kujawski wants to incorporate manipulatives into her high school geometry class for two units of study to improve students' conceptual understanding of geometric concepts. She attends a workshop on manipulatives and then writes lesson plans to include them. She tracks grades and uses word problems on a formal (graded) and informal (non-graded) basis to analyze student understanding over a 9-week period. Finally, she conducts a summative evaluation of her progress over the 9 weeks in

Other Examples of Process Portfolio Goals—continued

relation to this goal and adjusts and expands her manipulative program over the next 9-week period.

  2. Mr. Alexander wants to use graphic organizers in his high school English class. He develops four organizers to use over a semester and only uses them in two of his four 11th-grade standard English classes. His evidence compares the progress of two sections that used the graphic organizers with the two sections that didn't use them.

  3. Miss Cato is a chorus teacher at the high school level. To motivate her beginning chorus class, she wants to incorporate the use of hand instruments and rhythmic exercises and methods into her class. She uses these over a semester. Her reflection includes tracking participation, having students complete a self-evaluation on the process, and writing her own self-evaluation.

WHAT IS A PRODUCT PORTFOLIO?

A product portfolio is a specific set of evidence developed over a short period of time to meet a desired outcome. This type of portfolio is similar to a project. Each person developing a product portfolio has identical or very similar pieces of evidence. For teachers, product portfolios would be created around a particular goal or initiative. Teachers may create them to show how a school goal is being met, to seek a license, or to compete for an award. Any time teachers need to be compared using the same criteria, a product portfolio is a valid measure. This portfolio has specific, required evidence so developers can be compared consistently against the set criteria by assessors.

Product Portfolio

Each teacher is creating a portfolio to show the implementation of a schoolwide discipline program.

Purpose:
To document how each teacher participates in and supports the new schoolwide discipline approach

Audience:
Teacher and principal

Types of Evidence:
Listing of rules and procedures, copy of discipline log for each class (part of plan), parent contact log, parent conference record, motivation incentives

Placed in:
An expandable folder

Using writing again, a teacher's product portfolio could be developed to show the implementation of the "writing process" in the classroom (steps including brainstorming, draft writings, editing, revising, and final draft of the written product). Imagine that a district sets a goal that each teacher will use the writing process in his or her classroom, regardless of the subject(s) taught. The purpose would be to show how a teacher implements the writing process into day-to-day classroom activities, lesson plans, unit plans, and student assessment methods. For example, each portfolio could contain staff development information, lesson plans, unit plans, and student work demonstrating each step of the writing process and assessment rubrics or checklists. Reflections would include descriptions of how the writing process was included in the classroom, the strengths of and improvements needed for implementing the writing process, and how changes would be made during the next lesson or unit. All portfolios developed would be assessed using the same criteria, probably by the principal in this example.

EXAMPLE 1

Sample Product Portfolio

Background:
Jane Goodman, a middle-level educator, teaches science to students in the seventh grade. As part of a district initiative, all science teachers are implementing a lab-based curriculum. It is a prescriptive curriculum that includes a teacher's manual with lab procedures for the entire school year (one concept per week for 28 weeks).

Purpose:
To document the implementation of the lab-based science curriculum across the district

Audience:
District science supervisor

Organization:
Notebook divided into 28 sections

Evidence:
Student work samples and lesson plans are included for each of the 28 sections.

Reflection:
Ms. Goodman writes a reflection at the end of each week and at the end of the school year.

Sample Product Portfolio—continued

Assessment:
The district supervisor reviews the portfolio. In addition, the supervisor interviews Ms. Goodman and holds small-group conferences with clusters of teachers. The portfolio is used as the basis for these assessment activities. The results of these conferences, interviews, and portfolio contents allow the district supervisor and teacher to set goals for the next year.

Why Is a Product Portfolio Chosen?
The district supervisor chose a product portfolio because she wanted to compare how teachers implemented the new curriculum. By choosing a product portfolio, she can see the strengths and weaknesses of individual teachers and the curriculum as a whole.

EXAMPLE 2

Sample Product Portfolio

Background:
Suzi Greene and Gwen Stowe are high school Spanish teachers who teach Spanish 1 at All Good High School. As part of a district initiative, Spanish has become a required subject to meet the district goal of having all graduates become bilingual. It is a mandate that all students, regardless of background and desire, take Spanish. As a result, many of the students in the class are unhappy about taking Spanish. In addition, the class has a wide range of experience with Spanish—students with no background, those who had Spanish in middle school, and native speakers. Of course, this creates a unique teaching situation for these two veteran teachers, who had students who took the course as an elective in the past. They decided to create a product portfolio with identical evidence to determine the success of three subsets of students: native speakers, those who had some middle school background and would have elected to take Spanish, and those who were given Spanish as a mandate based on district policy. Of course, all three of these subsets could be found in each class period.

Purpose:
The main purpose was to assess the attitudes and achievements of all students in Spanish 1 classes. The plan was to use three proven strategies along with peer tutors in the class (a new idea for these teachers). In addition, attitudinal surveys would be taken. The portfolio will be developed over one semester, because the high school is on block scheduling.

Sample Product Portfolio—continued

Audience:
Mrs. Greene and Ms. Stowe with the results shared with their department chair

Organization:
Hanging crate with different sections for different classes and three files within each section for subsets of students within each class (students with middle school background, native speakers, no middle school background)

Evidence:

1. Student work from the use of each of the three proven strategies divided by three subsets
2. Teacher data sheet showing grades based on different strategies (copy of grade book with strategies highlighted in three colors)
3. Teacher reaction about student motivation and participation based on each of the three strategies. This reaction is done in two ways: overall and by using three subsets.
4. Copy of peer teaching procedures
5. Peer teachers' (native speakers') written responses to the peer teaching program
6. Tutored peers' written responses to the peer teaching program
7. Student Attitude Informal Survey Results by subsets

Reflection:
Mrs. Greene and Ms. Stowe wrote their own reflection and then analyzed students' responses to the peer tutoring program and its strategies.

Assessment:
Because the purpose of the portfolio is to improve the instruction and attitudes of students, data were analyzed by subsets (by strategy), and attitudes were analyzed by the categories positive, negative, and neutral. Results from the surveys and grades helped Mrs. Greene and Ms. Stowe determine which strategies were effective in motivating students. The peer teaching model was reviewed by the three stakeholders: teacher, peer tutor, and the peer who was tutored. Results were summarized and presented to a department chair at a meeting by the two teachers.

Why Was a Product Portfolio Chosen?
Mrs. Greene and Ms. Stowe chose a product portfolio so they could compare "apples with apples" in relation to strategies and peer tutoring. By choosing a product portfolio, they could see the strengths and weaknesses of each strategy and the peer tutoring model as a whole and analyze each component by subgroups.

Other Examples of Product Portfolios

1. Mrs. Williamson wants to analyze her students' progress using authentic assessments in eighth-grade algebra over one unit of study. She develops three authentic assessments, reflects on their impact, does an analysis of the students' grades, and has the students write a reflection about connecting math to life.

2. Erin Gray is a business teacher who teaches an introduction to desktop publishing class. The state has revised the curriculum to include a goal that focuses on the development of authentic ads for the school and community. Teachers are required to turn in a small portfolio to assess the implementation of this authentic goal in the curriculum. This is a new challenge for Erin, a second-year teacher. She develops relationships with the different booster clubs within All Good High School and has her students develop 10 ads for the different booster organizations over a 6-week period. These will appear in the school newspaper and on posters around the community. As required, she keeps a copy of each of the ads, writes about the development and success of this goal, has an evaluation sheet from each booster organization, and includes student reflections on the development of real ads.

3. Mr. Guidry uses a product portfolio to assess the yearly progress of his students' U.S. history grades by goal in comparison to state or national tests that evaluate the same goals.

EXAMPLE 3

Sample Product Portfolio

Background:
Thomas Adams and Gabriella Pinto are in their first education class at A+ University. They are going to be visiting schools and doing specific educational assignments at their schools.

Purpose:
To document the education assignments required for their Education 100 class (Introduction to the School)

Audience:
Instructor, Dr. Mark L'Esperance

Organization:
Three-ring binder divided into five sections with a cover page

Evidence:
Five specific assignments along with a reflection for each assignment

Sample Product Portfolio—continued

1. School tour and technology assessment write-up
2. Teacher observation
3. Student interview (at lunch)
4. Teacher interview
5. Ten-minute student activity

Reflection:
One for each of the five assignments plus a final reflection

Assessment:
Portfolio is assessed by Dr. L'Esperance

Why Is a Product Portfolio Chosen?
Because students do specific assignments, the product portfolio is the natural choice. The portfolio design allows students to begin to understand the reflective piece and the organization of a portfolio that is required later in the program.

WHAT IS A SHOWCASE PORTFOLIO?

Showcase portfolios are collections of a person's best work, chosen by the individual. These portfolios are often used for job interviews or teacher-of-the-year competitions. The purpose of the portfolio is for a teacher to showcase his

Showcase Portfolio

A high school math teacher is searching for a job. He creates a showcase portfolio.

Purpose:
To obtain employment in teaching

Audience:
Potential employers

Types of Evidence:
Sample lesson plans, classroom management plans, teaching evaluations, college transcripts, letters from students and student teaching supervisors, philosophy of education paper, resume, pictures of students taught, videotape of teaching, sample student work

Placed in:
Three-ring notebook

or her best work in one or more areas. For example, the teacher could develop a showcase portfolio to prepare for a teaching award. The portfolio would contain evidence chosen by the developer. This evidence would be what the developer believes to be his or her best work in teaching. Some developers might place several best lessons in his or her showcase portfolio, whereas another teacher might add a series of lessons that highlight various teaching strategies. Reflections for any showcase portfolio would focus on why evidence was chosen and why it is deemed best work. The main idea of this portfolio is that the developer chooses what to showcase and how to organize it. Unlike the other two types, this portfolio is completely individualized and is based on the perceptions of the developer about himself or herself.

EXAMPLE 1

Sample Showcase Portfolio

Background:
Mark Smith is a business education teacher looking for a high school teaching position.

Purpose:
To obtain a teaching position

Developer:
Mr. Smith

Organization:
The evidence is collected in a three-ring binder under four areas determined by Mr. Smith: teaching, management, computer skills and knowledge (since this would be an integral part of the business curriculum), and involving parents and the community.

Evidence:
Mr. Smith would include sample evidence under each area. This includes: lesson plans, unit plans, student work, videotapes and pictures of teaching, resume, philosophy of education position paper, management plan, classroom rules, sample work using different computer software including processed documents showing word processing skills and spread sheets, samples of letters sent to parents, and a parent communication plan.

Reflection:
One is written for each area. Mr. Smith answered the following questions: (1) Why was the evidence chosen? and (2) What are the strengths of the work?

Assessment:
By the person who interviews Mr. Smith

EXAMPLE 2

Sample Showcase Portfolio

Background:
Katlyn Easley, Elyse Bullock, and Cathy Stang are all middle school teacher candidates. They all attend A+ University, which is noted for its teacher education program. As part of their internship, they are required to create a product portfolio based on specific middle school standards for teaching.

Purpose:
To document that each intern can meet specific middle school standards for teaching based on their best work. Interns choose their best work to meet standards.

Audience:
The interns (Katlyn, Elyse, and Cathy), their supervising teacher, and their university advisor

Organization:
Notebook is divided into three sections based on three specific goals. One reflection for each goal is based on specific guided questions.

Evidence:
Evidence for each goal
    Goal 1 (instruction): unit of instruction, student work, pre–post data, reflection
    Goal 2 (classroom management): discipline plan, case study tracking three adolescents with specific discipline issues and their resolution.
    Goal 3 (social and emotional development): three character education lesson plans that specifically focus on social and emotional development along with student work

Reflection:
One for each goal and then an overall reflection at the end

Assessment:
The clinical teacher and university advisor review the portfolio. In addition, the clinical teacher and university advisor both write a reaction to the showcase work.

Why Is a Showcase Portfolio Chosen?
A showcase portfolio allows the candidates to compile their best work and build on that for job interviews.

WHAT ARE THE DIFFERENCES IN THE THREE PORTFOLIOS?

All three types of portfolios are purposeful collections of evidence with thoughtful reflections. The difference between the portfolios revolves around three components: (1) the purpose of the portfolio, (2) what type of evidence is collected, and (3) how the evidence is collected. The "what" and "how" of evidence collection is a direct result of the portfolio's purpose. For example, in a process portfolio with a purpose of showing the progress of teaching skills, the "what" of evidence would be a collection of documents that show the obtainment of teaching skills, while the "how" would be the developer's choice. For the product portfolio with the purpose of demonstrating the use of a specific teaching strategy, the "how" and "what" are the same for all developers. In a showcase portfolio with the purpose of highlighting a teacher's best teaching skills, the "how" and "what" of evidence are both determined by the developer.

Check for Understanding

It is important for readers of this book to develop an understanding of content prior to moving to the next section. Use the following questions to check comprehension:

1. What are the three types of portfolios?
2. What are the differences between the three types?
3. What are the four common components of all portfolios?
4. Give an example for each type of portfolio.

If all questions were answered correctly, you are ready to move on to the next section. If all answers were not clear, reread part or all of this section.

DIFFERENT TYPES OF PORTFOLIOS FOR ELEMENTARY TEACHERS

Table 2–1 gives readers an opportunity to compare how the three types of portfolios can be used to demonstrate a school goal.

TABLE 2–1   *Different Types of Portfolios for Elementary Teachers*

Background: An elementary school has implemented a new reading program. The principal has decided to require teachers to build portfolios in relation to the reading program. This chart shows how each type of portfolio can be used in relation to the new program. The teachers are the developers. All three types of portfolios, process, product, and showcase, are identified, with the four components outlined for each.

Type	Purpose	Audience	Sample Evidence	Reflection Focus
Process	To show the teacher's individual growth in using the new reading program over 1 year	Principal, Teacher*	1. Lesson plans showing reading program being implemented 2. Student work 3. Audiotapes of various students reading once a month for the school year 4. Running records showing successful and struggling students' progress over the year 5. Parent conference write-ups indicating the new program had been implemented	For each piece of evidence, the teacher could describe how it is related to the reading program and the strengths and weaknesses of implementing the program.
Product	To show that each teacher had implemented specific components of the reading program	Principal	Specific components outlined by the principal at the beginning of the year. Each teacher would have the same types of evidence; e.g., all teachers might be required to have lesson plans showing the correlation to the reading program.	The teacher would focus on the strengths of the required evidence.
Showcase	For teachers to show their best work in relation to implementing the reading program	Principal	Teachers would choose evidence that shows their best attempts at implementing the reading program. This could include: 1. Effective lesson plans 2. Excellent student work 3. Running records of students who showed great progress	The teacher would reflect on each piece of evidence, emphasizing the strengths of the evidence in relation to the reading program.

*For improving teaching

WHAT IS A TEACHING PORTFOLIO?

Portfolios, in general, are used by professionals in many different types of careers. A teaching portfolio is specific to the education profession. Shulman (1994) defines a teaching portfolio as "a carefully selected set of coached or mentored accomplishments substantiated by samples of student work and fully realized only through reflective writing, deliberation, and serious conversation" (p. 8). Painter (2001) sees a teaching portfolio as a documented history of a teacher's learning process viewed against a set of teaching standards. Successful development of a complete portfolio is through the deliberate selection of evidence and thoughtful reflections on those artifacts, which provide insight into teachers' growth.

Teachers can develop portfolios at any stage of their careers. McNelly (2002) states that portfolios can be used to gauge teacher effectiveness and student achievement, changing teacher evaluation processes from narrow to broad and deep. This can begin with preservice teachers at the university level who are preparing to enter the profession and progress to those who are master teachers who choose to apply for national board certification. A teaching portfolio contains evidence that shows the knowledge, skills, abilities, and dispositions of a teacher at his or her particular stage of development. The portfolio is usually organized around the central components of teaching, including planning and teaching a curriculum, student-centered instruction, student development, strategies, assessment practices, classroom management procedures, and professional development opportunities. The portfolio can take on many different shapes and sizes. The quality should be based on the depth of the evidence and reflection. Evidence in a teacher's portfolio would minimally include lesson plans, classroom procedures and management plans, sample tests, student work, professional conference materials, committee work, and parent contact logs. For each of these entries, a written reflection would be included.

A teacher's portfolio is a useful component for a teacher at any stage of development. Preservice teachers are acquiring the skills and knowledge to teach in their college or university program. Through a portfolio, they can document their acquisition of knowledge of teaching and their ability to teach. University faculty can have preservice teachers reflect on their emerging abilities and knowledge. Over the 2 to 3 years preservice teachers are in their teaching programs, their views and concrete knowledge of teaching change quickly. Evidence and reflections can help document the rapidly changing views and knowledge of a preservice teacher.

Once preservice teachers complete the required components of their teacher education program, they enter the induction phase of their careers. The induction phase encompasses the 1st to 4th years of a teacher's career. During this period, the teacher is commonly called a beginning teacher. At the onset of this stage, most beginning teachers have a probationary license, which allows them to teach during this trial period.

In the initial phase, teaching portfolios are used for licensure purposes or reemployment. In this portfolio, beginning teachers create portfolios that document their ability to teach effectively. At the end of their probationary period (length determined by each state), beginning teachers move from holding an initial license to a continuing license (one that is renewable with course or workshop credit every 5 years or so). At this time, teachers usually have tenure. For a continuing teacher, the teaching portfolio becomes an option to demonstrate professional growth based on personal needs or interests. For example, a teacher might be interested in learning more about children's learning styles (Dunn & Dunn, 1978) and implementing this theoretical approach in his or her classroom. In his or her teaching portfolio, evidence would include information about learning styles and examples of implementing this approach in the classroom. Evidence could include the new classroom layout showing learning styles centers, lesson plans emphasizing the approach, and classroom procedures that support the change. Portfolios for professional development are an option to traditional evaluation methods for teachers, such as observations by principals. Continuing teachers have tenure, so the portfolio option frequently becomes their choice. However, in some states, portfolios are used as an assessment tool for teacher licensure renewal. These cycles are usually 5 years in length.

Once teachers have taught for 5 years or more, they usually enter the next stage of their careers—the master teacher stage. The master teacher is one who would have the skills, knowledge, and beliefs reflected in the National Board standards. These teachers can choose to apply for National Board certification through the NBPTS. The successful teaching portfolio compiled for National Board certification demonstrates how the teacher is ranked against a set of standards in his or her field. At this stage, the teaching portfolio is an option for teachers.

No matter what stage a teacher is in, a teaching portfolio can be developed. The purpose of the portfolio changes at each stage of a teacher's career. However, at each stage the portfolio would contain evidence related to teaching and reflections that outlines the teacher's knowledge, abilities, and beliefs. Figure 2–1 lists examples of portfolio evidence. Refer to different chapters in this book for information and examples of teaching portfolios at different levels.

• Lesson plans	• Teacher projects
• Unit plans	• Classroom rules
• Philosophy of education paper	• Parent communication
• Pictures of classroom activities	• Team newsletters
• Videotapes of lessons taught	• Professional development certificates
• Student work	• State curriculum correlation with lesson plan
• Differentiation methods for exceptional children	• Pacing guides
• Case studies	• Test preparation strategies
• Action research projects	• Listing of motivation strategies
• Lesson plans showing varied teaching and learning strategies	• Grading policies
• Planning guides	• Department or grade-level meeting minutes
• Copies of a lesson plan book	• Committee memberships
• Community involvement	• School newsletters with highlights of class accomplishments
• Photos of student performances	• Field trip information (with students)
• Letters from students and parents	• Classroom floor plans
• Photos of student work	• Technology competencies of the teacher
• Workshops attended (certificates)	• Peer reviews
• Position papers	• Self-evaluations
• Student projects	• Professional development plans
• Parent volunteer information	• Transcripts
• Classroom organization strategies	• Volunteer work (teacher)
	• Related work experience

Compiled by the authors from a review of more than 300 portfolios

FIGURE 2–1 Types of Portfolio Evidence

Check for Understanding

1. What is a teaching portfolio?
2. How is a teaching portfolio different from other professionals' (i.e., artists') portfolios?

LEGAL ISSUES IN PORTFOLIO DEVELOPMENT

No teacher can create or design a teaching portfolio without reviewing the legal parameters. Teachers, in particular, are sensitive to children's rights and want to portray an image of doing the right thing in relation to the privacy issues of their students. The rule of thumb for legal issues is to look at the audience. If the audience is someone besides the developer, immediate supervisor (i.e., principal), or state licensing agency, have the students' parents sign a release form allowing their children's work to be included in the portfolio. Many school districts have release forms on file. The legal ramifications for parent release vary from state to state and district to district. Check this out carefully

Sept. 1, 2005

Dear Parents,

    I am a student teacher in Mrs. Adams's class at Bright Days Elementary School. As part of my college requirements, I am creating a teaching portfolio. I would like to include sample work from your child. Your child's name will not appear on any work included or in the written text describing it. Your signature below allows me to include your child's work in my portfolio. Thank you for your support. Feel free to contact Mrs. Adams if you have any questions.

                Sincerely,

                Ms. Lee

I give permission for my child's work to be included in Ms. Lee's teaching portfolio.

Parent's signature _____

Date_____

FIGURE 2–2   Sample personalized release form

with your school. Teachers should also send an informational letter explaining the purpose of the portfolio. Figure 2–2 provides an example of a letter. These two items can be combined, as seen in the sample. If the developer is submitting the portfolio to his or her immediate supervisor or to a licensing agency, no release forms are needed. The bottom line for teachers should be to rule on the side of conservatism. Assume that you need release forms from outside reviewers even if your colleagues don't think you need them.

    While the release form is the mainstay for legal defense, the following guidelines are good to follow to uphold the ethical rights of teachers, especially if the audience is external:

1. Mark out all students' names.
2. Refer to students anonymously in reflections.
3. Don't identify students in pictures.
4. Be sensitive about children with special needs. Don't include them by name or by picture in a portfolio.

    The best advice is to first check school policies regarding legal issues and, second, to use common sense when deciding about types of evidence. Many people who read this section will think that there are more legal issues related to portfolios. There are very few laws related to this, but there are ethical guidelines that should be followed.

Videotaping is another area of legal consideration, because school districts require a release for videotaping. These releases should be kept on file by the teacher. Students whose parents would not give permission should *not* be included in the videotape. According to federal law, children with special needs should not be videotaped.

Check for Understanding

1. When must you use a release form?
2. What are the ethical guidelines to follow when building a portfolio?

GENERAL CONSIDERATIONS FOR DEVELOPING A PORTFOLIO

After a teacher decides on the purpose of his or her portfolio, there are some general guidelines, regardless of his or her stage of development. Further information for specific teacher stages are described later in the book. General guidelines include:

1. **Save Everything.** Either keep evidence in a box in the classroom (throw it in) or create files for different types of evidence.

2. **Choose a Container.** Portfolios can be placed in three-ring notebooks, file boxes, or folders. Notebooks are the most common types of containers used by developers.

3. **Customize for External Reviews.** Use plastic sheets to house evidence. This will give the portfolio a professional look and keep evidence neat.

4. **Create a Professional Cover.** This will give a reviewer his or her first impression. The developer's name and picture are minimal components. Inspiring quotes, clip art, borders, and a title (for a professional portfolio) add character to the cover page.

5. **Organize the Portfolio.** If the portfolio is developed for external audiences, a table of contents is key. Tabbing different sections allows for easy access. These small features allow reviewers to easily view the contents.

6. **Begin with an Introductory Section.** Developers should include a section on themselves that includes a resume and other pertinent information, such as letters of reference and a statement of philosophy.

7. **Word-process Everything.** Cover sheets, sections, tables of contents, tabs, and so forth should *not* be handwritten. A professional appearance is important.

8. **Spelling and Grammar Are Very Important.** Developers should use standard English and proofread their work. Enlist help from a colleague if needed. Again, professional work is important.

9. **Videotapes Should Be Heard.** If a videotape is chosen or required as evidence, a developer should make sure that his or her voice is heard when taping. Although the videotape does not have to be professional, *hearing* the

teacher is important. Enlist a colleague to help with the videotaping. Videotape can also be transferred to a CD easily if the videocamera is a digital brand. By using a CD, snippets of the teaching episode can be placed on different tracks.

10. **Videotape Technical Tips.** Use a tripod, check for glare, have light in the background, do a sound check, and cut off extraneous sounds. Consider a practice run to check for these things.

11. **Videotape Content.** Tapes should be watched to make sure "purpose" has been met. Watching the tape from a teaching and learning perspective will allow developers to "see" the taped episode from both the teacher's and students' views.

CLOSING THOUGHTS

This chapter has given readers an overview of types and general logistics of portfolio development. The portfolio is a powerful assessment tool for teachers. Its ability to "tell the story" of the developer allows for depth and breadth that isn't possible through any other medium. Specific portfolio types allow teachers to choose evidence around a defined purpose, resulting in an effective product.

CHAPTER ACTIVITIES

1. List and describe the components of portfolios and the different types of portfolios.
2. Give examples of information (types of evidence) that would be included in each type of portfolio.
3. Apply the information you know about the types and components of portfolios to describe a situation when a specific type of portfolio would be useful and the reasons why or how.
4. Using information in your own classroom and your experiences, what information from your classroom, teaching, and planning could be included in a portfolio, and how would it strengthen the portfolio? What would be demonstrated by including those items?
5. Choose evidence from your classroom and teaching and classify that evidence into different categories to fit into each type of portfolio.

WEB SITES

Teacher Portfolio Contents Examples
http://www.uwosh.edu/career/portfolio.html

REFERENCES

Adams, T. L. (1995). A paradigm for portfolio assessment in teacher education. *Education, 115,* 528, 658–570.

Campbell, D. M., Cignetti, P. B., Melenyzer, B. J., Nettles, D. H., & Wyman, R. M., Jr. (1997). *How to develop a professional portfolio.* Boston: Allyn & Bacon.

Dunn, R., & Dunn, K. (1978). *Teaching students through their individual learning styles: A practical approach.* Upper Saddle River, NJ: Prentice Hall.

Krause, S. (1996). Portfolios in teacher education: Effects of instruction on preservice teachers' early comprehension of the portfolio process. *Journal of Teacher Education, 47,* 130–138.

McNelly, T. A. (2002). Evaluations that ensure growth: Teacher portfolios. *Principal Leadership* (Middle-level ed.) *3*(4), 55–61.

Painter, B. (2001). Using teaching portfolios. *Educational Leadership, 58*(5), 31–34.

Shulman, L. S. (1994, January). *Portfolios in historical perspective.* Presentation at the Portfolios in Teaching and Teacher Education Conference, Cambridge, MA.

Tierney, D. S. (1993). *Teaching portfolios: 1992 update on research and practice.* Berkeley, CA: Far West Laboratory for Educational Research and Development.

Wolf, K. (1996). Developing an effective teaching portfolio. *Educational Leadership, 53*(6), 34–37.

CHAPTER 3

Reflection

Reflection is the key component in portfolio development. It requires developers to think about what they are doing, why they are doing it, what the outcomes are, and how the information can be used for continuous improvement (McLaughlin & Vogt, 1998). The absence of a written reflection results in a portfolio becoming a scrapbook. Reflections are a crucial component in portfolio development. They tell the reader what the developer values about his or her teaching. Scanlan and Chermomas (1997) describe the process of reflection based on the premise that it facilitates understanding of self in relation to practice. The written words that comprise a reflection allow readers to hear the developer's voice in relation to evidence included in the portfolio.

Heinrich (1992) states that reflection is a process by which the teacher can develop his or her own voice in the evaluation of professional practice. Essentially, the reflection is the "glue" of the portfolio—it gives substance to the collection and guides the reader. In fact, it is reflection that allows any individual to improve and grow. The role of reflection in portfolio assessment complements the idea of the teacher as a reflective practitioner. Reflection is seen as a significant component for professionals. The emphasis on teacher reflection grows out of a body of literature that emerged during the 1980s and describes the need for, approaches to, and benefits from reflection (Cady, 1998; Sparks-Langer & Colton, 1991). As educators engage in instruction and then reflect on it, the process offers insights into various dimensions of the teaching and learning process that can lead to better teaching (Schon, 1987). If professionals never reflected on their actions or beliefs, improvement of practice would be minimal or nonexistent.

WHAT IS REFLECTION?

Reflection is the process of looking at information or events, thinking about and critiquing them, and then using the results to change or enhance future events. The process of reflection facilitates the understanding of self in relation to practice (Scanlan, Care, & Udod, 2002). In teaching, reflection on their own practice and on the achievements of their students is done consistently by teachers. Each day, reflective teachers think about what they have done and how they can do it better. While engaged in the teaching act, a master teacher is already "redoing" a lesson plan based on the responses of students and their ability to meet the objectives. Figure 3-1 illustrates that teaching reflections consist of three vital components: (1) description, (2) analysis, and (3) future impact.

To begin the process of reflection, a *description* is important. The description should emphasize the following: who, what, when, where, and how. The description component provides the foundation for the rest of the reflection. This is an important segment for the audience of the portfolio. If a clear description is provided, the other two components will be easier to write. For a beginning teacher, being able to describe the segments of an executed lesson will allow him- or herself to think about the process of teaching. For many beginning teachers, lessons are a whirlwind experience where they are trying to teach while managing student behavior and procedures, presenting new content, and using new methods while motivating students and remaining enthusiastic. The process of formal reflection allows these educators a chance to break down their lessons into sections, beginning by describing the process of the lesson.

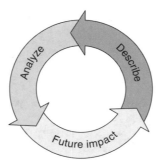

FIGURE 3–1   The Teacher's Reflection Cycle

Three Stages of Reflection	
Description	Future impact
Analysis	

Reflection 1: Sample Description by a Preservice Teacher

This piece of evidence is a math lesson on "volumes of prisms, cylinders, pyramids, and cones" taught to a seventh-grade class with a diverse population of students with varied learning abilities. Things considered when planning this lesson were (1) the prior knowledge of the students and (2) the fact that the class has children who become disengaged easily. As a result of these factors, I filled my lesson with various activities that required participation. During my planning, I developed pictures and models for students so they would understand the concept I was teaching.

When teaching this lesson, I took on the role of a coach. I gave instruction and allowed students time to do the activities, and informally assessed students during the activities. I looked at students' body language, facial expressions, interest, effort, and ability to get the "right" answer. If they seemed to have interest, positive body language, and an ability to get the "right" answer, I would move on in the lesson. However, if they failed to exhibit these things, I would reteach, review, or give another example for them to work on. This choice was based on the signals I received from the students.

This math lesson addressed the state math curriculum goal, "demonstrate an understanding and use of measurement." I did this by instructing students how to measure the volume of geometric figures like cylinders, prisms, and cones. In the lesson, I used both pictures and models to give students a representation of the abstract concept of volume. This helped those who were visual and kinesthetic to receive instruction in a form they could easily understand.

What is a plus/delta T chart?

This is a simple process tool that allows a person to visualize his or her strengths and areas to improve.

$$+ \qquad\qquad\qquad\qquad | \qquad\qquad\qquad\qquad \Delta$$

Next, the developer will *analyze* the evidence. Analysis means to break the whole apart and look for patterns. Patterns can be looked at in terms of strengths and areas to improve. In this section, the strengths of the evidence are outlined along with areas on which to improve. The plus/delta T chart is an excellent tool to analyze lessons. For example, if a lesson plan were included, the developer would outline the positive components of the plan and its implementation, and then emphasize areas on which to improve for the next lesson plan. Teachers who write thoughtful reflections are honest about their own strengths and weaknesses. Some evidence, such as a workshop certificate, may not require developers to reflect on how they would improve from it. The developers themselves will have to determine if the certificate is relevant as a piece of evidence.

Reflection 1: Sample Analysis by a Preservice Teacher

The lesson's success can be addressed from two perspectives. One, the lesson was successful because students participated, and through informal assessment, they seemed to understand the content addressed within the lesson. Two, the lesson was not successful because it did not cover all the content and I insisted on perfection. The content was not covered in a very efficient or effective manner. I seemed to dwell on drilling the students on concepts they already understood, which took away from quality instruction time. I also insisted on perfection from students on each aspect of the lesson before I was willing to move on to the next one. Therefore, I ran out of time before all content was addressed.

The final stage of reflection, *future impact*, is perhaps the most important. In this stage, the developers write about how the evidence has affected them and the implications for the future based on this evidence. The future impact section allows educators to outline future teaching plans based on this reflection.

Reflection 1: Future Implications by a Preservice Teacher

Teaching this lesson taught me that assessment was necessary, that drilling was not necessary, and to set my goals at an achievable level for students. Through this teaching experience, I saw firsthand how assessment was essential in good teaching. It is essential because it allows instruction to be centered around what students know and what they need to know. I learned that assessing students within a lesson can help pinpoint the instruction method that works best with the content, environment, and students. Second, I found that drilling was not necessary. I discovered that it is boring for students because they are not challenged to think for themselves but simply repeat back what others have already thought through. In the future, I plan to informally assess students in a way that would allow them to think through, for themselves, the content I am teaching. Third, I want to set achievable goals for students. In this lesson, I almost set my students up for failure because the achievement level I expected of them was mastery. I realized that very few people will become "masters" of a content area. Therefore, I should not set my students up for mastery, but rather for the attainment of an achievable goal. In this lesson, I should have emphasized their ability to think through a problem as my achievable goal for the lesson. Instead, I resorted to a mastery level, where students had to correctly answer each

Reflection 1: Future Implications by a Preservice Teacher—continued

informal assessment topic before being able to move on to any other content instruction. I do not think that extremes are essential; however, I do believe it is necessary for students to have a good understanding of a content area before moving on to related content areas. I think this is necessary so that proper background understanding can be formed by the student. This will allow new content understanding to more easily be established in a student's mind.

Overall, I was extremely pleased with the lesson plan, the teaching experience, and the outcomes that the lesson brought in both the students' content understanding and my own professional understanding.

After reading this entire reflection, there are a few things that stand out:

1. It is written in the first person. This is appropriate for any reflection written for a portfolio because the reflection is a personal account of the evidence and reactions to it.
2. The reflection is an accurate description and goes beyond superficial analysis.
3. It is well written. The reflection is clear and there are no grammatical and spelling errors. Writing well is a difficult task. When reflections are well written, it adds quality to the portfolio.
4. The content is accurate and honest. Reflections should provide an accurate description and analysis of the evidence. The previous reflection shows the teacher's ability to write about her strengths and weaknesses in connection to teaching the lesson plan. This provides insight into her development as a professional. If the reflection were superficial, it would be less informative and effective.

WHY SHOULD TEACHERS REFLECT?

Reflection is deemed an important component of the teaching profession. The Interstate New Teacher Assessment and Support Consortium (INTASC), National Board for Professional Teaching Standards, and Pathwise (Praxis III) formalized the expectations for teaching reflection (Cady, 1998). One of the five tenets of National Board certification is the ability to reflect on practice. The tenet states, "Teachers think systematically about their practice and learn from experience." National Board certified teachers are models of educated persons who strive to strengthen their teaching. These nationally certified teachers critically examine their practice and use this information to change or enhance it (National Board for Professional Teaching Standards, 1996). In addition, most preservice teacher education programs incorporate reflection into each class. At this stage, preservice teachers use reflection to develop skills, knowledge, and abilities. Inservice teachers use reflection to refine teaching skills and demonstrate their practices during evaluation sessions with principals and supervisors. These examples show how reflection is seen as a vital component of each stage of teacher development. As teachers engage in reflection, they become more thoughtful about their practice, and consequently, they become more effective teachers.

Reflection teaches that there is no such thing as failure, only the development of personal insight from one's experiences. To be reflective means to mentally wander through where one has been and try to make sense of it. This includes drawing cognitive and emotional information from all sources, linking experiences to previous learning, comparing results that were anticipated and intended with the results that were achieved, and searching for answers (Costa & Kallick, 2000).

Check for Understanding

1. What are the three components of reflection?
2. Why is reflection important for teachers?
3. What role does reflection play in portfolio development?

WHAT THINGS SHOULD BE CONSIDERED?

There are four areas to consider before writing a reflection: audience, clear writing, voice, and bias. These should also be used as a checklist after writing a reflection.

Audience   When writing a reflection, first consider your audience. The developer should be aware of the audience at all times. If the audience is a potential employer, the reflection should be written with principals or other supervisors in mind. Knowing the audience allows the developer to write purposefully.

Clear Writing   Second, write clearly. A reflection that is well written will enhance any portfolio. Pay specific attention to grammar and spelling. It is especially important for teachers to write clearly because it is a skill that is expected. When writing reflections, record thoughts first and then edit. Appropriate professional language should be used for any reflection written.

Voice   Third, the voice of the reflection should be that of the developer. The reflection should be written in first person, since it is a personal reflection.

Therefore, the use of *I* and *me* are appropriate. When the reflection is read, it should be clear that the developer is expressing his or her thoughts.

Bias   Fourth, be sensitive to ethnic groups, gender, and children with special needs when writing a reflection. Use politically correct terms for all ethnic groups and sensitive language when talking about children with special needs. It is important for the teacher to present him- or herself as a professional and to not offend any audience member who would read the portfolio.

Bias is often a difficult topic for many people to discuss openly. When reading other people's writing, preconceptions and stereotypes around diversity can interfere. For example, a teacher might give the demographics of his or her classroom (e.g., *the class had 14 Caucasian students and 13 African American students*). To many readers, the listing of ethnic percentages might seem commonplace in today's schools, but other readers might see the "listing" of ethnic percentages as biased because it labels certain groups of children. It is helpful to have someone else read reflections to review for bias.

HOW DO YOU GET STARTED? DO THESE REFLECTION ACTIVITIES!

The best way to write good reflections is to begin by looking at models of good and bad reflections and analyzing them in terms of strengths and weaknesses. Read each of the following reflections and analyze them in terms of (1) the stages of reflection and (2) the four areas to consider, previously outlined (audience, clear writing, voice, and bias.)

Directions for Analyzing Reflections

Read the reflection.

1. Using a plus/delta T chart, indicate the strengths and things to improve on in relation to the reflection cycle (description, analysis, and future impact) and the four areas to consider (voice, audience, clear writing, and bias).
2. Give the reflection a holistic score based on the following:
   - + +   Outstanding, exceeds in all areas
   - +   Well done, all criteria met
   - +/−   Some criteria good, other criteria needs improvement
   - − −   Poorly done, needs improvement in most areas

For the first scoring opportunity, reread the reflection given earlier in this chapter and estimate how you would score it using the holistic scoring guide (++, +, +/−, − −). See Appendix A for the author's response to this reflection.

Now read the following two reflections on a science lesson and a video-taped lesson, and follow the same directions to analyze and score them.

Reflection 2: A Science Lesson

[Description] I taught a science lesson to a group of seventh-grade boys and girls from diverse ethnic backgrounds. Most of the students in this class are struggling, and several are repeating this grade. The behavior of many of the students was challenging. The lesson focused on simple machines. I began by having the students write a few notes on what they knew about simple machines. Then we brainstormed together about things we see everyday that might be simple machines. Everyone was involved in the discussion. Next, I spent 15 to 20 minutes describing each of the six simple machines and demonstrating with models. The students were able to watch, reflect, and then work with the machines. We discussed as a large group, worked in small groups that I supervised, and reflected individually about what we wrote, saw, and touched. In addition, I encouraged vocabulary building and note taking, using a handout that we completed together. During the time left at the end of class, the students worked on hidden word puzzles I created just for this lesson.

Since I have taught this class for several weeks, I was very aware of the importance of keeping the students involved, of keeping the lesson going, and of constantly reinforcing the information in a variety of ways (discussion, hands-on, note taking, and games). I wanted the information to be accessible. I gave illustrations of simple machines using things the students are familiar with. I was pleased when one child made the connection between an inclined plane and ramps for wheelchairs at the hospital where his mother works, and when another student made the connection between a pulley and an elevator. During the lesson, all the students were interested in handling the simple machines that I brought in. Some of the definitions and equations took more time than I anticipated, so I had to skip the "independent practice" section of my lesson plan, but I thought it was important to teach how simple machines are a part of our everyday lives.

[Analysis] I used the textbook as the lesson's foundation, but I constructed my own teaching props, and there was a good deal of interest because of the immediacy of the subject matter. The lesson was very

Reflection 2: A Science Lesson—continued

successful. My students were even able to reduce some complicated machines in the world around them to simple terms. Science helped them to explain the world. I showed them that science is useful and that it is valuable because it is useful. The least effective part of the lesson was the puzzle, because it was not clear enough to be useful as a reinforcement tool. I had to do more explaining than I wanted to. Overall, the class was not quiet during the lesson, but much of the noise was constructive. For the most part, my students all stayed on task. The lesson probably included a little more information than could be efficiently mastered in one lesson. The introduction of the simple machines alone, without definitions and equations, would have been more than enough, but, all in all, the lesson was a positive experience for me and for my students.

[Future impact] The experience showed me the value of making academic information relevant and real (see, feel, touch, hold). This class is very social and active, and this type of lesson lent itself to group interaction and discussion. I was able to use these strategies effectively because I was prepared. Maintaining control of the classroom is easier when students are interested, and it is up to me as a teacher to help them see why they should be interested. It is necessary to acknowledge where they are (their need for social interaction) and to recognize what tools will most efficiently get them to where I want them to be. This lesson reinforced the importance of preparation and appropriate teaching strategies based on the needs of my students and the information I am teaching.

Reflection 3: A Videotaped Lesson

[Description] This piece of evidence is a videotape of a lesson I taught to a general math class. The lesson was on two- and three-digit division in which I reviewed students for the standardized test. The videotape was a requirement for a class, but I am glad it was. It was required to allow me to evaluate myself teaching and to determine how effective the lesson was. It was taught using an overhead projector, and the students also worked out problems on the chalkboard. The strategy used for teaching the lesson was mini-lecture. The cooperating teacher wanted me to teach the lesson this particular way.

A videotape of a lesson relates to teaching because a teacher should constantly evaluate him- or herself to see how effective the lesson was and

Reflection 3: A Videotaped Lesson—continued

what, if any, changes can be made. A teacher should be a reflective practitioner who continually assesses the effects of his or her choices and action on others. This helps the teacher grow professionally. He or she should also use the videotape to teach the same lesson at a later date.

[Analysis] I believe the lesson went all right, but it could have gone better. Some students participated, but others didn't. The students were alert mostly because they knew the lesson was being videotaped. They also knew that their teacher was watching them [the cooperating teacher]. While I was teaching, I felt as if the lesson was somewhat effective, but after watching the videotape, I felt differently. The students were bored with the lesson. Some were yawning and others had their heads down.

One strength of the lesson was that the students seemed as if they knew the material I was teaching or that the lesson was a review for the standardized test. Those who did participate knew all the answers and could work the problems independently. But there were several weaknesses in the lesson. One weakness was that I wasn't aware of what was going on around me. When viewing the video, I saw students talking, yawning, and even passing notes. Evidently, the students did all of these things while I was working our problems on the overhead. This really irritated me.

[Future impact] In the future, I need to be more creative with my lessons. The plans should be more student-oriented. I know from this experience that overhead projectors will be of minimal use in my classroom, and when I use them, the students will teach the lesson using the projector. When I start teaching, I don't think that I will lecture a lot to my students either.

As a teacher, I have to be aware of the classroom environment. Students will take advantage of you if you let them, and they will also do things behind your back. I have to move around my classroom to make sure the students are on task. This videotape really helped me and I'm glad that we were required to do it.

WHAT ARE SOME THINGS TO DO TO GET STARTED?

The process of reflecting becomes easier the more one does it. If this process seems overwhelming, try going through the following steps to help develop reflection skills for each of the three stages: description, analysis, and future impact.

Description   Begin by verbally describing events to another person. Below are some sample questions to ask or use as a guide. The questions this person asks during the conversation will help clarify and enhance the description. Practice this verbalization technique with a description of something passionate related to teaching, such as a great lesson, a child affected, or a great workshop attended. Once the reflection can be clearly articulated, it is time to write the description. There will probably be several drafts of the reflection. In the first draft, focus on getting the description down on paper. During the second draft, edit the reflection for grammatical and spelling mistakes. When reflections are done several times, the process will become easier.

Sample Description Questions	
Who was involved?	What was your role?
When did it happen?	What was the outcome?
What happened?	Where did it happen?
What are the details?	

Description Practice Prompts

Prompt 1:
Think about the best lesson that you ever taught. Describe it. Who was involved? Where did it happen? What was the objective of the lesson? What was its subject? What happened first, second, third?

Prompt 2:
Choose one of the best staff development workshops you have attended. Describe it. Why did you go? What material was covered? Who did the workshop? Where was it held?

Prompt 3:
Think about a child affected by your teaching. Describe him or her. Who is the child? What is he or she like? What impact did you have? What specific examples of the impact can you give?

If you are training to be a teacher, you might not have the classroom experience to do the prompts just described. Here are some beginning prompts:

Description Practice Prompts
for Beginning Teachers

- Describe the best teacher you ever had.
- Describe when you learned something new (how to drive, how to cook).
- Describe when you taught something to someone else (how to cook brownies, how to do a cheer).

Analysis   The process of analysis means that one must look critically at the evidence, break it into patterns, and determine the strengths and areas in which the developer needs to improve. This is a difficult task for some people because they must look critically at themselves and their own work. Begin by creating a plus/delta chart that can conveniently be made from a T diagram as seen below. On the "plus" side, write down all the strengths of the evidence. The "delta" side is where the improvements go. This simple chart provides for an organized way to begin the second stage of reflection. After the chart is completed, the first written draft of this portion of the reflection can be written. Again, the second draft is for editorial purposes.

Plus/Delta Chart	
plus	delta

Analysis Practice Prompts

Directions:
Write a reflection using the guiding questions below.

Prompt 1: Best Lesson.
What went well with the lesson? Why did you teach the lesson the way you did? Was the objective achieved? Was it planned well? What did students learn? What did students do correctly? Incorrectly? What did you do correctly or incorrectly?

Directions:
Write a second reflection using the prompting questions that follow.

Prompt 2: Workshop Attended.
What were the best materials of the workshop? What things did you learn? What things might you disagree with that were presented in the workshop?

Prompt 3: Child.
What positive impact did you have? What interventions were tried? What interventions worked? Which ones didn't work?

Analysis Practice Prompts for Beginning Teachers

- What were the strengths of the best teacher you ever had? What were the areas where this teacher could have improved?
- When you learned something new (how to drive, how to cook), what did you do best? In what areas did you need to improve?
- When you taught something to someone else (how to cook brownies, how to do a cheer), what did you do well?
- What could you have improved?

Future Impact   This component is the most important part of the reflection. If a teacher does not talk about how he or she will use the information, then the reflection is essentially useless to him or her or any other reader. It is this component that effects change in teachers' behavior and provides the intrigue for reading portfolios. A good way to begin this component of the reflection is to brainstorm effects of the evidence. A list may include 2 or 20 items. Once the list is brainstormed, write the first draft of this section. Then edit and rewrite until you are satisfied with the reflection.

Future Impact Practice Prompts

Directions:
Add to your practice reflections using the guided questions.

Prompt 1: Lesson Plan.
What will you do the same in the future based on this lesson? What would you do differently? What new strategies might you use? What strategies might you use again?

Prompt 2: Workshop Attended.
How can you use this information with your students? In your teaching? What goals could be set based on this new workshop information?

Prompt 3: Child.
What interventions could you use with other children? What interventions might you never use again? What impact did this child have on your teaching philosophy? How did your values change as a result of this experience?

Future Impact Prompts for Beginning Teachers

- How will the best teacher you ever had affect you as a teacher? What will you do that he or she did?
- How did learning something new (how to drive, how to cook) affect your life as an adult?
- How did teaching something to someone else affect your decision to become a teacher?

WHAT IF THIS SEEMS DIFFICULT?

One great tip is to recruit a friend to help with this process. A friend who is a teacher would be the best choice. Use this person to do peer reviews. Even great writers have someone edit their work. By sharing this experience with another professional, teachers can demonstrate and practice effective learning skills, probe for clarity and understanding, ask thoughtful questions, and share metacognitive thoughts. One way to do this is for colleagues to sit in a circle and have each person reflect on the day's activities. Another option is to have a recorder for the group or pair and not discuss activities until all events are written. Participants can then offer and analyze problems or share responses to the written text.

WHERE AND WHEN CAN YOU REFLECT?

One of the most difficult things for a teacher to do is find time to reflect. Reflection can happen in many places at many times. It is important to reflect in a physical place that is comfortable. If teaching episodes are used for evidence, it is important to reflect on them soon after the delivery of these lessons so details are clear to the developer.

Places and Times for Teachers to Reflect	
At the end of the day	During planning
In the car to and from school	At home

CLOSING THOUGHTS

Reflection practice develops over time. At first this might seem overwhelming and difficult, but it will be easier with time. Reflection brings a voice to portfolios—the teacher's voice. The voice makes the portfolio come to life for the reader and for the developer. In teaching, as in life, maximizing meaning from experiences requires reflection. Without reflection, a portfolio could not tell a teacher's story.

CHAPTER ACTIVITIES

1. What is reflection? Define and describe the three components of good teaching reflections.
2. How would reflecting help you better prepare for your students and your teaching in general?
3. Describe a time when reflecting would be useful to you, and how.
4. What time(s) during a school day would be best to reflect? Why, and how would you use this time?
5. Analyze one aspect (lesson, conference, etc.) of your teaching day and reflect on each piece of it. Determine things that you could change in the future and how changing those items might make a difference for your students' achievement.

WEB SITES

Learn North Carolina Web site concerning the reflection cycle
http://www.learnnc.org/newlnc/newteach.nsf/0/317C733AC3FFA11485256C8D007 2399C?OpenDocument

REFERENCES

Cady, J. (1998). Teaching orientation: Teaching. *Education, 118*(3), 459–471.

Costa, A. L., & Kallick, B. (2000). Getting into the habit of reflection. *Educational Leadership, 57*(7), 60–62.

Heinrich, K. T. (1992). The intimate dialogue: Journal writing by students. *Nurse Educator, 17,* 17–21.

McLaughlin, M., & Vogt, M. (1998). Portfolio assessment for inservice teachers: A collaborative model. In *Professional portfolio models: Applications in education.* Norwood, MA: Christopher Gorden.

National Board for Professional Teaching Standards. (1996). *Middle childhood/generalist standards for National Board Certification.* Detroit, MI: Author.

Scanlan, J. M., Care, W. D., & Udod, S. (2002). Unravelling the unknowns of reflection in classroom reflections. *Journal of Advanced Nursing, 38*(2), 136–144.

Scanlan, J. M., & Chernomas, W. M. (1997). Developing the reflective teacher. *Journal of Advanced Nursing, 25,* 1138–1143.

Schon, D. (1987). *Educating the reflective practitioner.* San Francisco: Jossey-Bass.

Sparks-Langer, G. M., & Colton, A. B. (1991). Synthesis of research on teachers' reflective thinking. *Educational Leadership, 48*(6), 37–44.

PART II

APPLICATIONS OF PORTFOLIO DEVELOPMENT

Chapters 1 through 3 contain background information for all readers. Now is the time to choose a specific direction; different chapters focus on portfolios for teachers at different stages of their careers. Chapter 4 is for preservice teachers, while Chapter 5 is for those who want to create a teaching portfolio for job interviews. Beginning and experienced teachers should read Chapter 6 to learn how to develop a licensure portfolio or if one is interested in using a portfolio as an alternate to traditional evaluation. Those who seek National Board certification should turn to Chapter 7. Chapter 8 provides practical information on a futuristic trend—electronic portfolios. There is information for teachers at every stage in this handbook.

Each chapter is organized in the same way. While that may seem repetitious, it allows the reader to immediately open to the chapter he or she is interested in and begin reading. This part of the handbook is not sequential. At the beginning of each chapter, there is an introduction. The purpose and audience for each type of portfolio is given, followed by organizational features. Sample evidence and assessment criteria are also identified. Following a general overview section, specific examples are provided for each type of portfolio. To help plan portfolios, guiding questions are also offered.

The Preservice Teacher's Portfolio

Preservice teachers are in the first phase of their professional career—the acquisition of a license to teach. For most individuals, teacher preparation occurs during their undergraduate preparation at a college or university. Students enrolled in teacher preparation programs create portfolios to demonstrate their knowledge, skills, and attitudes related to teaching.

Portfolios are created by preservice teachers for many reasons. Portfolio assessment of students has become increasingly prevalent in schools; it also has become more widely used in preservice teacher education programs (Barton & Collins, 1993). These include meeting program requirements or for personal reasons. Many times, requirements are outlined by university or college faculty; thus, the portfolio's purpose is often predetermined by the faculty in the preservice teacher education program. Even if a program doesn't prescribe a portfolio over time, preservice teachers may choose to create a portfolio for many different reasons. Over the course of a teacher licensure program, students develop many valuable skills and experiences related to teaching that are complex. A portfolio can help a professional make sense out of the multitude of experiences and knowledge acquired during a program. It can bring into focus a clear picture of an individual as a growing, changing professional. Most of all, it allows one to demonstrate to others skills, knowledge, and abilities related to teaching (Campbell, Cignetti, Melenyzer, Nettles, & Wyman, 1997).

All three types of portfolios—process, product, and showcase—can be created by preservice teachers even if they are not required by programs. The move toward performance-based assessment in teacher education programs across the nation is resulting in the requirement of portfolios in teacher education programs. Performance-based assessment, a result of standards-driven programs, requires prospective teachers to be assessed on what they know and are able to do (Interstate New Teacher Assessment and Support Consortium [INTASC], 1992).

Many teachers choose to create portfolios for their own professional reasons. Preservice teachers who would like to develop their reflection skills and want to increase their professional experiences should consider creating a portfolio. Using program requirements, or "outcomes," is a simple, direct way to organize a portfolio based on preservice education coursework. These outcomes, commonly called program goals, are a good organizational framework for preservice teachers developing a portfolio.

Sample Preservice Portfolios

Purpose:
Show that program requirements are met

Sample Requirement:
Writing and implementing a variety of lesson plans over a sequence of courses

Type of Evidence:
Lesson plans with reflections

Process:
A series of lesson plans are placed in the portfolio. Reflections focus on how each lesson plan was better than the last one.

Product:
Specific lesson plans and reflections are required for a portfolio.

Showcase:
Students would choose which lesson plans (or if any lesson plans) and reflections would be placed in their portfolios.

All three types of portfolios can be used to show program requirements. A **process portfolio** can be created that shows the preservice teacher's progress in a program during different classes. Evidence, with reflections, can be included from each class in the program. Over the entire program, preservice teachers create a portfolio that shows their abilities as a teacher in relation to the objectives of the program or each class. Specifically, through field experiences in a sequence of classes over four semesters, a program might have the goal of having students plan and teach a variety of lessons. In these field experiences, preservice teachers have to write lesson plans and teach them at their field sites. Students can then place these lesson plans and teaching reflections in their portfolios. In addition, the developers (students) reflect over time on the improvements in their teaching.

Another option is to create a **showcase portfolio** showing a preservice teacher's best work over the course of the program. Using the lesson plan example, each preservice teacher would choose which lesson plans he or she would include in the portfolio. Some students might include all lesson plans, while others might include only one. The key for the showcase portfolio is that each student chooses which evidence, in his or her opinion, best reflects program requirements, and includes it.

A third choice would be for preservice teachers to create a **product portfolio,** which contains specific pieces of evidence that reflect program outcomes. Again, using the lesson plan example, the program requires specific lesson plans and reflections be included in the portfolio. Each of these types of portfolios could be used for the purpose of demonstrating program requirements.

Another organizational design for a process or product portfolio model would be to use goals determined by the preservice teachers or a set of adopted standards or goals. Standards-driven portfolios are usually developed using adopted standards, such as those of the INTASC for beginning teachers.

WHAT DO THESE GOALS AND STANDARDS PORTFOLIOS LOOK LIKE?

Using personal or program goals or standards as an organizational framework, preservice teachers may develop a product or process portfolio to show the relationship between the goals or standards and the knowledge, skills, and abilities of a preservice teacher. If preservice teachers are demonstrating that they are meeting the goals, a product portfolio is the best choice. Process portfolios may be used if developers want to show evidence that demonstrates how skills, knowledge, and attributes related to each goal or standard are obtained (i.e., step-by-step).

TYPE 1: THE GOAL-DRIVEN PRODUCT PORTFOLIO

The purpose of this portfolio is to show that preservice teachers met the goals they developed. Since a developer is showing competence related to specific goals, a product portfolio would be the best choice. The audience may be preservice teachers or university or college faculty. This type of portfolio differs from other goal-driven models because the preservice teacher determines what goals will be demonstrated in the portfolio. Prospective teachers in the same program may have different goals. For example, one student may focus his or her goals on developing skills to work in a rural school. Sample goals for this portfolio might include (1) understanding and motivating the rural child, (2) working with multiple groups in the same classroom, and (3) developing strategies that integrate art and music into the core curriculum (i.e., in many rural schools, teachers are responsible for all subjects). Another student in the same program may be focused on technology in the classroom. Sample goals for this student may be (1) integrating technology in the classroom, (2) learning to use different types of software, and (3) facilitating student development through technology. Again, the key is that each student is responsible for setting and demonstrating the attainment of each goal. Since the portfolio is personal, the goals can be unique. Anyone interested in this type of portfolio may first want to think about what components of teaching most interest them.

Organization

The product portfolio is set up in accordance with the goals of the developer. Its length varies, depending on the type of goals and the audience for the portfolio. Those students who are in a 1-year teacher education program may have a smaller portfolio than those who are in education classes for 2 or 3 years. The portfolio is developed by preservice teachers. Feedback and direction regarding the appropriateness and direction of the portfolio may be sought from university instructors.

The format is simple. Depending on the number of goals, students divide the portfolio into the same number of sections. If there are five goals, there are five sections. The evidence is gathered from the classes and field experiences in the teacher education program. Developers may choose any type of evidence that is consistent with the goals.

Sample Product Portfolio Setup Using One Goal

Goal:
To teach effectively using a variety of strategies.

Developer:
Preservice teacher

Evidence:
(1) lesson plans showing a variety of strategies from various field experiences, (2) written observations from supervising teachers regarding performance from practicum experiences and student teaching, (3) a long-term plan for a unit taught during student teaching that shows a variety of strategies

Sample Product Portfolio Setup Using One Goal—continued

Organization:
Three-ring binder

Reflection:
Based on the question: How does evidence show that the goal has been met?

Assessment:
Oral and written feedback may be sought from university or college faculty at various times.

The developer's reflections would focus on how goals are met through the evidence. Assessment may occur through written review or oral feedback from faculty members. Other types of assessment could include peer review with other students and presentations and interviews with faculty members.

There are advantages and disadvantages for choosing this type of portfolio. Advantages include having clear, consistent goals driving the portfolio and having an easy format for organization. The major disadvantage is that this type of portfolio is determining the goals.

Questions to Ask Yourself if You Are Interested in This Type of Portfolio

1. What are the goals of your program? Sample goals include:

   - Effective teaching
   - Being able to manage students (classroom management)
   - Hands-on instruction
   - Professional growth
   - Knowledge of the subject matter

2. What goals would you like to demonstrate in your portfolio? Look at the list above (no. 1). Are any of these goals consistent with yours in relation to teaching? What other goals do you have? Think in broad terms.

3. What types of evidence would demonstrate each goal? Sample evidence includes lesson plans, student work, written feedback, compositions, journals kept during practicum experiences, professional activities, and units developed.

4. What type of physical organization would this portfolio have? The easiest organization is a three-ring binder divided by goals.

5. What is the role of university and college faculty? The faculty member could be a facilitator or an evaluator.

6. What types of reflections would you want to see in this portfolio? Would there be a reflection for each piece of evidence or for each goal?

Sample Goals-Driven Product Portfolio

Introduction:
Kelly Cave is a student in a preservice middle grades program. She will work with students in Grades 6 through 9 when she graduates. She is enrolled in a small teacher education program that is 2 years in length. During these 2 years, she has been in two practicum experiences and a semester-long student teaching experience. In addition, she has been in a series of middle-level coursework.

Goals (many reflect program goals):
Kelly's goals:

1. Plan lessons and units that match the state curriculum and meet the needs of adolescents
2. Integrate the curriculum using two or more subjects
3. Plan activities for adolescents that meet physical and psychosocial developmental needs
4. Develop classroom management strategies
5. Be involved in professional-development activities

Developer:
Kelly (a preservice teacher)

Purpose:
To demonstrate that goals are met

Organization:
Three-ring binder, organized by goals

Teacher's Story*:
I organized my portfolio by each goal. For organizational reasons, I bought a big notebook and a set of dividers. I kept all of my assignments and practicum information in a big cardboard box during the semester. In addition, I would write notes on each piece of evidence to include in my reflection. At the end of each semester, I would choose evidence to place under each goal. It was important for me to balance what I learned in class with my practicum experiences in the public schools. As I worked on my portfolio, I began to see the "big picture" of what I believed, knew, and would do as a teacher. This was an important assignment, in my opinion, because it forced me to reflect on what I had learned and take charge of organizing my thoughts and skills as a middle-level teacher.

*Reprinted with permission. Kelly Cave is now a successful teacher at Gentry Middle School in Surry County, North Carolina.

Sample Goals-Driven Product Portfolio—continued

How Did I Organize It?
I began by setting up the portfolio in a binder. As mentioned above, I used the "pile" method of organization—keeping all assignments and practicum paperwork in a cardboard box in the corner of my room. I would drop everything into the box when I got it back from the professor.

What Evidence Did I Include?
In the front of the portfolio, I placed a cover page that included my name, major, and a piece of clip art. Next came an organizational table of contents.
*The **first section** was an **introduction to myself,** which included my resume and an autobiography that I wrote in one of my classes. Following this were the five goals divided into sections.*

Order of Introductory Evidence

1. Cover page
2. Table of contents
   Introduction Section
3. Resume
4. Autobiography
   Goals by Sections

Goals and Evidence

Goal 1: To plan lessons and units that match the state curriculum and meet the needs of adolescents
Evidence: *A copy of the state curriculum; five different lesson plans with the correlated state goal and objective, plans that also reflect five different methods that are appropriate to use with adolescents; a unit plan (long-range); a videotape of myself teaching three of the lessons*
Goal 2: To integrate the curriculum using two or more subjects
Evidence: *Integrated unit prepared for methods class; integrated unit taught during student teaching experience; samples of student work of integrated assignments from the unit; informal surveys from students about the integrated unit*
Goal 3: To plan activities for adolescents that meet physical and psychosocial developmental needs

Evidence: *Intramural plan for students, observation of exploratory courses done in practicum, advisor–advisee curriculum (planned), activities taught during student teaching, and a case study of an adolescent conducted during the first year*

Goal 4: To develop classroom management strategies

Evidence: *Series of case studies done as coursework, semester-long observation record of class behavior, management plan for class, log of management record during student teaching, preliminary classroom rules and procedures for the first year of teaching*

Goal 5: To become involved in professional development activities

Evidence: *Agenda from a student middle school association meeting, list of professional organizations that I belong to, list of workshops attended during my student teaching experience, copy of PTA membership card*

A Moment to Think

1. Choose a goal. Divide a piece of paper into two columns.
2. In the left column, brainstorm, for 2 minutes, course assignments and school experiences that would fit under that goal.
3. Now, move to the right column. For each item in the left column, give a reason why it fits under the goal you have chosen. This part of the activity will help you with your reflection section.

Author's Reaction to Evidence

Kelly's evidence was appropriate for each goal. By choosing to place evidence under one goal, many things could have been repeated. For example, lesson plans can go under Goals 1 and 2, so Kelly must decide which type of plans she should put where. While a reader might disagree with her organizational decisions, the thing to remember is that *placing the evidence was her choice.* The keys to a successful goals-oriented portfolio are the selection of appropriate evidence and clear reflections that support the work samples.

Reflection

For each piece of evidence, a short reflection was written describing it and telling how it meets the goal. For each section, a longer cumulative reflection that encompassed all evidence and its relevance was written by Kelly. In the longer reflection, Kelly also focused on what she learned and how she would apply it to her teaching philosophy.

Sample Short Reflection for Goal 1
Evidence: Copy of State Curriculum

This is a copy of the math curriculum for our state. It is expected that I will teach the content of this curriculum in sixth grade. I have included this under Goal 1 because it shows that I understand there is a state curriculum that I am to follow when formulating lesson plans and units.

Assessment:
At the end of the first year, I asked for informal feedback on my portfolio. There were three categories in which written feedback was given by faculty members: (1) content, (2) reflections, and (3) organization and general feedback. Based on the feedback received the 1st year, I revised my portfolio for the 2nd year. This interim feedback was valuable for me; it allowed me to see that I was on the right track.

At the end of the second year, I had the option to present my portfolio to a group of peers and university faculty. I used the evidence from each goal to summarize in a 20-minute presentation how I met each goal. Then I answered questions. This was a powerful experience. I had to take everything I had done over 2 years and summarize it. This experience made me think about each goal individually and how to link them together. I reflected on everything that I had put together over the 2-year period, reread all of my reflections, and wrote a summary based on all of them. I didn't receive a grade for my portfolio. I did it for myself. I would not trade this opportunity for any other.

Author's Reaction to Reflection

This type of portfolio allows for personal growth on the part of the preservice teacher. By the time Kelly was finished with her portfolio, she understood herself better and grew as a teacher as a result of this experience. The most valuable outcome is her ability to reflect on her experiences.

Using a Rubric to Evaluate This Portfolio

A holistic rubric could be used to evaluate this portfolio. The rubric would have to be general in nature, since developers would determine their own goals. Here is an example of a holistic rubric for a goal-driven portfolio:

Outstanding   The portfolio has clear, articulated goals. The evidence is related to the goal and shows that the goal is clearly met by the developer. The reflection intertwines the evidence to show how the goal is met and how the developer has grown as a result of setting and reaching this goal. Overall, the goal was clearly designed and met.

Good   The portfolio has clear goals. The evidence is related to the goal and supports it. The reflection uses the evidence to explain to what extent this goal was reached. The candidate learned from setting the goal. Overall, the goal was met, but there was room for more reflection and learning for the developer.

Moving Toward Competency   The portfolio developer has set goals and gathered evidence that support their attainment. There is a reflection written on the goal. There is a lack of evidence, or the reflection doesn't show clearly how the goal was met. Overall, there are "holes" of some type in the portfolio.

Doesn't Meet Competency   There isn't a clear connection between the goal(s), evidence, and reflection. Overall, the goals aren't met.

TYPE 2: THE STANDARDS PORTFOLIO

A standards portfolio in preservice teacher education is developed using a set of standards as the organizational guide. Any type of standards can be used to develop a portfolio. These can be chosen from the Interstate New Teacher Assessment and Support Consortium (INTASC standards) or any national organization, such as the National Middle School Association or the National Council for Teachers of Mathematics. The majority of teaching organizations have developed standards. These can be readily organized and assessed.

In this chapter, the INTASC standards have been chosen because they outline good teaching principles for any teacher at any stage in his or her career. Any set of standards can replace them, and the same portfolio organizational pattern can be used.

INTASC Standards*

The INTASC standards were developed by a group of educators from states that belong to the Interstate New Teacher Assessment and Support Consortium under the auspices of the Council of Chief State School Officers. The purpose of these standards is to assess the knowledge, skills, and abilities of beginning teachers. In 1987, the Council of Chief State School Officers established a consortium to enhance collaboration among states interested in rethinking teacher assessment for initial licensing as well as for preparation and

*From *Model Standards for Beginning Teacher Licensing, Assessment, and Development: A Resource for State Dialogue.* Copyright 1992 by the Council of Chief State School Officers. Used with permission.

induction into the profession. This consortium came about as a result of re-structuring efforts for America's schools. High school graduates are being required to perform at higher levels to perform in the workforce, thus demanding changes in the curriculum. Rather than merely "covering the curriculum," teachers are expected to find ways to support and connect with the needs of all learners. These learner-centered approaches to teaching require change in teacher licensure, the vehicle for providing consistency in the type of teacher who enters the classroom. The INTASC standards have been adopted in over 17 states as a consistent measure for teacher licensure and competency (INTASC, 1992).

Preservice teacher programs have adopted the INTASC standards for two reasons: (1) the NCATE, the accreditation organization for schools of education, have incorporated the INTASC standards into its outcomes; and (2) schools of education want to compare their students against the standards for beginning teachers, since this is the outcome of teacher preparation programs. Following is a description of the standards, with specific indicators outlined for each as adopted by the consortium. The authors provide sample evidence for each standard.

Confronting INTASC

© Thomson 2000

Describing the Standards

Standard 1—Content Pedagogy   *The teacher understands the central concepts, tools of inquiry, and structure of the discipline(s) he or she teaches and can create learning experiences that make these aspects of the subject matter meaningful to students.*

Evidence should show that instruction is consistent with state curriculum guidelines, the curriculum is supplemented with external resources, the methods of inquiry are used, and the central concepts and tools of inquiry of the discipline are evidenced in planning.

Sample Evidence:

- Lesson plans that correlate with the state curriculum and include external resources: lesson plans that show state curriculum goals and objectives and/or district goals
- Units of study (integrated and interdisciplinary): a series of lesson plans around a central topic, concept, or theme that show connections between different subjects around the central focus
- Inquiry lesson plans: lessons that are built around a central question with the teacher playing the role of facilitator; students are not told answers, but are led to them through experiences.

Standard 2: Student Development   *The teacher understands how children learn and develop, and can provide learning opportunities that support their intellectual, social, and personal development.*

Evidence should show that you can plan or assess the link to students' prior knowledge; the encouragement of reflection on prior knowledge and its connection to new information; the integration of learning with other disciplines or real-world experiences; experiences for students that are appropriate for their social, emotional, and cognitive development, and provide opportunities for learners to be responsible for learning.

Sample Evidence:

- Lesson plans: any subject
- Manipulatives used: tangible items that explain concepts specifically used in mathematics
- Photos: of students, activities, or group work
- Developmental checklist: showing the growth of students against developmental criteria in different areas, usually done in early childhood programs
- Varied strategies used (lesson plans and units): lesson plans and handouts visualizing types of teacher and learner strategies used in the classroom
- Floor plans of the classroom: a graphic representation of how the classroom is set up, which includes desks, learning centers, and bulletin boards

Standard 3: Diverse Learners *The teacher understands how students differ in their approaches to learning and creates instructional opportunities that are adapted to diverse learners.*

Evidence should include adaptations of instruction to meet the needs of varying learner styles and the strengths and needs of learners (time and circumstances of work, the tasks assigned, and communication modes), and the incorporation of cultural contexts within the community.

Sample Evidence:

- Differentiated lesson plans: plans showing how assignments and strategies are changed or extended to meet the needs of all learners
- Videos of student performances: videotapes of speeches, projects, and the participation of students
- Learning centers: self-managed work centers set up around tables or desks where students investigate in a particular area
- Bulletin boards: artistic work around a theme on a flat wall board

Standard 4: Multiple Instruction Strategies *The teacher understands and uses a variety of instructional strategies to encourage students' development of critical thinking, problem solving, and performance skills.*

Evidence should include the use of multiple teaching strategies for challenging critical thinking (questioning activities), examples of how students are encouraged to identify learning resources, and the use of multiple instructional strategies (the teacher as facilitator, coach, instructor, or audience).

Sample Evidence:

- Video showing higher order questioning, activities, and assessments
- Explanation of grouping procedures: write-up explaining the levels in the classroom and how critical thinking is done with all students
- Collection of pre- and posttest data: test data showing how students did prior to and after a lesson, concept, skill, or unit is taught
- Planning based on students' differentiated abilities: lesson plans showing how all students' needs are met

Standard 5: Motivation and Management *The teacher uses an understanding of individual and group motivation and behavior to create a learning environment that encourages positive social interaction, active engagement in learning, and self-motivation.*

Evidence should include procedures and rules for classroom management; examples of the ability to organize and manage time, space, and activities conducive to learning; examples of the ability to analyze and adjust the classroom environment to enhance social relationships; illustration of student motivation and engagement, and examples of ways students are organized for various types of instruction (i.e., small and large groups, and cooperative learning).

Sample Evidence:

- Management plan: classroom rules and consequences
- Incentive system: student rewards
- Parent communication: letters, notes, phone calls, progress reports, and other ways parents are contacted
- Cooperative activities: lesson plans and pictures that show how students work together in cooperative ways
- Classroom procedures: how papers are turned in, pencils are sharpened, questions are answered, and other general processes

Standard 6: Communication and Technology   *The teacher uses knowledge of effective verbal, nonverbal, and medial communication techniques to foster active inquiry, collaboration, and supportive interaction in the classroom.*

Evidence should include the ability to model effective, culturally sensitive communication, support of learner expression (speaking, writing, and other media), and use of a variety of media communication tools to enrich instruction and learning.

Sample Evidence:

- Video: teaching showing motivation and communication
- Student evaluations: information from students about classroom environment and teaching
- Lesson plans showing uses of technology: lessons showing technology as a teaching or learning strategy
- Communication to parents and students: written documents such as syllabi and letters showing communication between the teacher and others

Standard 7: Planning   *The teacher plans instruction based on knowledge of the subject matter, students, the community, and curriculum goals.*

Evidence should include long-range units and daily lesson plans based on curriculum goals, adjusted plans based on unanticipated sources of input or learner needs, and appropriate plans for curriculum goals, diverse learners, and problem solving.

Sample Evidence:

- Short-term and long-term objectives: specific outcomes for each day, week, month, or year
- Pacing guide: an outline of what is taught when throughout the school year
- Unit plans: a series of lessons around a central theme or concept

Standard 8: Assessment   *The teacher understands and uses formal and informal assessment strategies to evaluate and ensure the continuous intellectual, social, and physical development of the learner.*

Evidence should include the use of a variety of assessment strategies; use of assessment strategies to adapt and adjust instruction; acquisition of information about students' learning behavior, learning needs, and the students themselves; useful records of student work and performance; and the involvement of learners in self-assessment to inform them of their strengths and needs and to encourage goal setting.

Sample Evidence:

- Formal tests: standardized test scores for classroom or school
- Work samples: student work showing a variety of students' abilities and types of assessments done in the class
- Writing samples: students' writing
- Authentic work products: projects, products, and other real-life work done by students
- Records of student and parent conferences: logs, records, and team logs of conferences

Standard 9: Reflective Practice: Professional Growth   *The teacher is a reflective practitioner who continually evaluates the effects of his or her choices and actions on others (students, parents, and other professionals in the learning community) and who actively seeks out opportunities to grow professionally.*

Evidence should include the evaluation of the self and self-improvement.

Sample Evidence:

- Attendance at professional meetings and presentations: programs, handouts, or materials received at professional meetings
- Attendance at workshops: staff development agendas
- Articles read or reviewed: summary of articles read, especially with ideas that are implemented
- Committee work: listing of committees served on in school
- Volunteer hours: work done with students on "own time" and other contributions to the school at large, beyond the regular day
- Journals: personal journal about one's teaching experience

Standard 10: School–Community Involvement   *The teacher fosters relationships with school colleagues, parents, and agencies in the larger community to support students' learning and well-being.*

Evidence should include documentation of participation in school activities, communication with parents, and consultations with other professionals on behalf of students.

Sample Evidence:

- Home visits: logs or records of home visits
- Knowledge of community agencies: summaries or explanations of links between agencies and students and schools
- Parent communication: sample letters and logs

Developing an INTASC Portfolio

The purpose of this portfolio is for preservice teachers to show they have the knowledge, skills, and ability to successfully teach as outlined in the INTASC standards. The developers are teacher education students. These students may get university or college faculty to serve as codevelopers. The audience is varied, depending on the purpose of the portfolio. It can include university or college faculty or the preservice teacher. It is organized according to the 10 standards. Reflection emphasizes a description of evidence that shows how standards are met and the impact on students' development. Assessment can be done in a variety of ways, both formally and informally. Interviews, written reflections, peer reviews, presentations, and blind reviews can be used. Informal interviews and feedback with university or college faculty members and the students' peers can only strengthen the portfolio process.

Questions to Ask Yourself if Interested in This Type of Portfolio

1. What standards will I adopt?
2. What role will I allow faculty to play in the development of the portfolio?
3. Over what time period will the portfolio be developed? One semester? One year? Two years?

FIGURE 4–1   Whitney Lawrence, student intern, confers with her clinical intern, Linda Freeman, about her portfolio.

The following sample shows how a university department adopted an INTASC standards organizational design. Individual preservice teachers could adopt this model or use a more general design where they show how standards are met throughout their program. One option would be to create a standards portfolio during the student teaching experience.

Sample Process Portfolio Design Using the INTASC Standards

The East Carolina University elementary and middle grades department has adopted a process INTASC portfolio model. The portfolio documents the development of preservice teachers against the INTASC standards over a 2½-year period. The faculty chose the portfolio as one means of assessing students because it is a type of authentic assessment that allows students to illustrate their learning through multiple forms of evidence and reflect on it. The portfolio is seen as a working document that preservice teachers can build on as they move into their professional lives as teachers.

Purposes of Portfolio:
This portfolio has three purposes:

1. Its first and primary purpose is to be a vehicle for thoughtful and knowledgeable reflection on the relationship between the preservice teacher's work and the INTASC standards.
2. The second purpose is to demonstrate growth of knowledge and skills that lead to effective teaching. These will be presented in the form of evidence categorized by the INTASC standards.
3. Its third purpose is to aid in the further understanding of portfolio processes and applications.

Organization:
A process portfolio is one that shows growth over time. During the 2½ years students are in the program, the focus is on the development of a process portfolio—one that shows the preservice teachers' growth in the profession over their time in the program. Each student keeps his or her portfolio in a three-ring binder and begins it in sophomore year. It culminates in the senior year.

Developer(s):
Preservice teachers with assistance from faculty in the department

Audience:
University faculty

Sample Process Portfolio Design Using the INTASC Standards—continued

Reflection:
Students write reflections for each piece of evidence. They describe the evidence and its relevance to the INTASC standard and detail how it affects their teaching.

Assessment:
At the end of each of the five semesters (from second-semester sophomore year to second-semester senior year—graduation), students turn in the portfolio to one instructor who is predetermined. A tracking sheet is kept in the portfolio, and informal feedback is given to the student each semester. A minimum of five pieces of evidence is required for each standard by the end of the program. The portfolio counts as a participation grade (approximately 10%) in each class. At the end of the senior year, after the student teaching experience, students turn in their portfolios for a final review. A two-way conversation is held between the university supervisor and the preservice teacher. A visual overview of the portfolio process for this program is shown below.

Middle Grades Education Sample Course Sequence Correlation with INTASC Standard

Course	Class/Semester	Standard(s)
Introduction to major	Sophomore second semester	Introduction to Standards
Introduction to preadolescent and middle school students	Junior first semester	1, 2, 3, 4, and 9
Curriculum and strategies	Junior second semester	1, 2, 3, 4, 7, and 9
Classroom management, curriculum, and assessment	Senior first semester	All
Internship/student teaching	Senior second semester	All

Evidence

The one criteria for the portfolio is that students include a variety of evidence with a wide range of media. As students move through the sequence of classes, different INTASC standards are emphasized. This will help students include evidence from each standard. What follows is a student sample using this organization.

Order of Introductory Evidence

1. Creative cover page
2. Resume
3. Ten standards dividers

Sample INTASC Student Process Portfolio

Introduction:
Russell Vernon is a student in a large middle-level teacher education program. He will teach in Grades 6 through 9 when he graduates. He is in the last semester of his program (second-semester of senior year). Two and one half years ago, he began his INTASC portfolio in his first major course. Over the span of five semesters, he has turned in his portfolio five times for informal reviews.

Standards used:
INTASC

Developer(s):
Preservice teachers

Purpose:
For preservice teachers to demonstrate they meet the INTASC standards

Organization:
All students organize their portfolios according to the 10 standards. Each student in the program is expected to divide a three-ring binder into 10 sections. Developers decide what evidence to include in the portfolio, but a minimum of five pieces are added each semester.

Teacher's Story*:
During my first education course, we were introduced to the INTASC portfolio model. At first, I was overwhelmed. Even though the instructor did a good job of introducing the concept, the first time I turned in my portfolio I didn't know what to expect. I was very anxious about the feedback that I would receive. After my portfolio was reviewed, I was glad that feedback was given. The next semester, we added five more pieces of evidence. This time I felt more confident when I turned in my portfolio. In my senior year, my portfolio went through a major transformation. I began to get really serious about what I was adding and how it would look to potential employers. During this phase, I pulled out much of the evidence that I had added earlier in my program and replaced it with samples collected during my internship [student teaching]. Overall, I feel that compiling the portfolio is a great experience for anyone. I learned that I had the skills and abilities to be a good teacher and could see the growth I made over the 2½ years.

*Reprinted with permission. Russell Vernon is now a successful teacher in Rockingham County, North Carolina.

Sample INTASC Student Process Portfolio—continued

How Did I Organize It?

I was required to set it up according to the 10 standards. This was easy to do. I chose evidence as I went through the courses and added it to my portfolio. Once I made a decision to add something, I went ahead and put it in my binder [portfolio]. I am a linear person, so this system worked for me.

What Evidence Did I Include?

Before the 10 standards, I placed a creative cover sheet with my name and major, and on the second page, a resume. In front of each divider, I wrote out the entire standard.

Evidence:

Standard 1: Team simulation demonstration that shows an intern working on an interdisciplinary team, shadow study, journal entries

Standard 2: Media analysis collage (the impact of media on adolescents), classroom environmental study, journal entries, case study

Standard 3: Concept web, adolescent profile, lesson plans showing different strategies

Standard 4: Team simulation, interactive bulletin board, integrated unit; videotape, photos of students in cooperative learning groups

Standard 5: Classroom rules, description and analysis of different discipline problems during the internship, classroom procedures, philosophy of management (essay)

Standard 6: Letter to parents during the internship, journal entries, phone log, project assigned with directions (to parents and students), parent conference summary sheet, technology assignments (with disk) done for a university class

Standard 7: Long-term planning guide, lesson plans, plan book, unit goals, objectives and rationale taught during internship

Standard 8: Pre- and posttest data, tests, projects, student work, copy of grade sheet

Standard 9: Journal entries, supervising teacher feedback sheet, dialogue journal used during internship

Standard 10: Committees served on during internship, conferences attended over 2½ years (agendas), workshop agendas

Reflection:

For each piece of evidence, I wrote a reflection. In these brief reflections, I would show the connection to the INTASC standards and give a brief description of the evidence. In addition, through two presentations, I was required to summarize my beliefs about teaching.

Sample INTASC Student Process Portfolio—continued

Assessment:
At the end of every semester for five semesters, I was given informal feedback on my portfolio. In my senior year, I was required to present my portfolio twice (at the end of both semesters). By this point, I was ready to present my evidence and be asked questions about my beliefs, knowledge, and skills. These opportunities allowed me to really think about what I believe and also what I would say in an interview. The portfolio was a requirement in the program. Each semester, it was given a participation grade using a checklist, and during my internship semester it was a requirement. If I had not completed it, I would have received a lower grade in my internship.

Author's Reaction to Evidence

Russell did a good job using a variety of media in his portfolio, including videotape, photographs, and various assignments from courses and school experiences. He could have more evidence showing his knowledge of content, something that is very important for a middle-level teacher.

Sample Reflection

Evidence:
Profile of an adolescent

Written:
First semester, junior year (second semester of portfolio development)

Reflection:
This entry was placed under Standard 3 because it proves that I have acquired an understanding of how students differ in their approaches to learning and the changes that occur during the adolescent years. This assignment helped me prepare for the future as I venture into middle schools.

Author's Reaction to Reflection

This type of portfolio also allowed for personal and professional growth. University faculty could use the evidence to review program outcomes and the effectiveness of their teaching majors. The entire process allowed for confidence building in students and reflection time for faculty.

Sample Standard Portfolio
Showcase Portfolio Design Using State Standards

Students at Sunnydale College of Education who are candidates in the secondary English program create a showcase portfolio based on six state standards for teachers in their state.

State Standards
1. The teacher has knowledge of content.
2. The teacher creates and maintains a learning climate.
3. The teacher implements and manages instruction.
4. The teacher assesses and communicates learning results.
5. The teacher reflects and evaluates teaching and learning.
6. The teacher collaborates with colleagues, parents, and others.
7. The teacher engages in professional development.

The portfolio documents the development of preservice teachers against the state standards over the year-long internship. The faculty chose the portfolio as one means of assessing students because it is a type of authentic assessment that allows students to illustrate their learning through multiple forms of evidence and reflect on it. This portfolio method is seen as an assessment where preservice teachers can use authentic products to show their knowledge, skills, and dispositions related to state standards.

Purposes of Portfolio:
This portfolio has two purposes:

1. Its first and primary purpose is to document and demonstrate competencies based on the best work of the preservice teacher.
2. The second purpose is to demonstrate knowledge and skills that lead to effective teaching. These will be presented in the form of evidence categorized according to the state standards.

Organization:
A showcase portfolio demonstrates the best work of an individual. During the year-long internship, candidates select evidence that demonstrates knowledge and skills in relation to state standards. Each student keeps his or her portfolio in a three-ring binder, and it is under construction for the 9-month internship.

Developer(s):
Preservice teachers with assistance from a cooperating and supervising teacher in the school

Audience:
University faculty

Sample Standard Portfolio Showcase Portfolio Design Using State Standards—continued

Reflection:
Candidates write reflections for each of the six standards. They describe the evidence and its relevance to the state standard and detail how it affects their teaching.

Assessment:
At the end of the internship experience, candidates turn in their portfolios for review. A two-way conversation is held between the university supervisor and the preservice teacher, and there is an assessment using a holistic rubric.

ASSESSMENT

One of the most important areas to take into consideration when developing a portfolio is to consider how it will be assessed. Preservice teachers may face a variety of assessment methods. If portfolios are developed for personal reasons, no assessment methods will be utilized. Individuals who are developing them as part of a program requirement will have them assessed.

What Assessment Methods Could Be Used?

Interview   A popular way to assess portfolios is by using a one-on-one or small-group student interview. During the allotted time, developers present key evidence that shows the major components of the portfolio. If it is a standards-driven product, one should be prepared to outline how each standard is met. Preparing for the interview is quite easy. Developers should review their portfolios so they are familiar with the location of different components and their content. Sample interview questions include: What have you learned in this program? What does the portfolio show me [the interviewer] about your teaching? How did you show that standard X or goal Y is met? What are your strengths? In what areas do you still need to improve? This is a time-consuming method for teacher education faculty.

Presentations   A twist on the one-on-one interview, the presentation, is usually done in front of faculty and peers. Given an allotted amount of time, developers should be prepared to present an overview of their program, giving highlights from different sections. Overheads or visuals may be helpful to facilitate this process. In the presentation, students are generally asked to give

FIGURE 4–2   Whitney Lawrence, student intern, reviews evidence for her professional portfolio.

an overview. Lasting 10 to 30 minutes, the end of the presentation is usually a time for questions from the audience. Be prepared to answer specific questions about the evidence presented, your strengths, areas to improve, and skills and knowledge learned throughout the program.

Written Evaluation   Another option is a written reflection that summarizes the contents of the portfolio or analyzes your views about the document or process. This method allows you to be reflective and in-depth about your feelings, views, and the artifacts in the portfolio. An excellent method to encourage written expression and reflection, it might be combined with one of the above methods. Write honestly and ask someone to proofread your work if this component is required.

Checklists and Rubrics   If developed for a grade, checklists or rubrics may be one of the assessment methods. Specific criteria related to the purposes of the portfolio will be outlined, and students' abilities to meet these criteria will be judged (see Table 4–1). Many times, after many informal assessments, rubrics or scoring criteria will be done during the last assessment of a process portfolio. Checklists (see Table 4–2) provide developers with cut-and-dry information about their ability to meet evaluation criteria.

TABLE 4–1   *Sample Rubric for INTASC Portfolio*

	Excellent	Good	Needs Improvement
Standard 1	The standard is clearly met through the choice of appropriate evidence and reflections that clearly show how the evidence intertwines with the standards. The developer meets each part of the standard clearly and consistently.	The standard is met through the choice of appropriate evidence and a reflection that shows how the standard is met. The standard is met (overall), but there may be components that are met more clearly than others.	There is evidence for this standard. The evidence doesn't clearly show that the components of the standard are met, or there is a reflection but it may not clearly show how the standard is met.
Standard 2	The standard is clearly met through the choice of appropriate evidence and reflections that clearly show how the evidence intertwines with the standards. The developer meets each part of the standard clearly and consistently.	The standard is met through the choice of appropriate evidence and a reflection that shows how the standard is met. The standard is met (overall), but there may be components that are met more clearly than others.	There is evidence for this standard. The evidence doesn't clearly show that the components of the standard are met, or there is a reflection, but it may not clearly show how the standard is met.
Standard 3	The standard is clearly met through the choice of appropriate evidence and reflections that clearly show how the evidence intertwines with the standards. The developer meets each part of the standard clearly and consistently.	The standard is met through the choice of appropriate evidence and a reflection that shows how the standard is met. The standard is met (overall), but there may be components that are met more clearly than others.	There is evidence for this standard. The evidence doesn't clearly show that the components of the standard are met, or there is a reflection but it may not clearly show how the standard is met.
Standard 4	The standard is clearly met through the choice of appropriate evidence and reflections that clearly show how the evidence intertwines	The standard is met through the choice of appropriate evidence and a reflection that shows how the standard is met. The standard is met	There is evidence for this standard. The evidence doesn't clearly show that the components of the standard are met, or there is a reflection

	Excellent	Good	Needs Improvement
	with the standards. The developer meets each part of the standard clearly and consistently.	(overall), but there may be components of the standard that are met more clearly than others.	but it may not clearly show how the standard is met.
The criteria at each level would repeat for Standards 5 through 10.	Repeat	Repeat	Repeat

TABLE 4–2 *A Checklist for Evaluating an INTASC Standard Portfolio*

Standard 1	Standard 2	Standard 3
__Evidence matches standard __Reflection develops standard __Standard is met	__Evidence matches standard __Reflection develops standard __Standard is met	__Evidence matches standard __Reflection develops standard __Standard is met
Standard 4	**Standard 5**	**Standard 6**
__Evidence matches standard __Reflection develops standard __Standard is met	__Evidence matches standard __Reflection develops standard __Standard is met	__Evidence matches standard __Reflection develops standard __Standard is met
Standard 7	**Standard 8**	**Standard 9**
__Evidence matches standard __Reflection develops standard __Standard is met	__Evidence matches standard __Reflection develops standard __Standard is met	__Evidence matches standard __Reflection develops standard __Standard is met
Standard 10	**Overall Evaluation**	**Overall Evaluation**
__Evidence matches standard __Reflection develops standard __Standard is met	Pluses:	Things to improve:

Person evaluating portfolio: _____

CLOSING THOUGHTS

In this chapter, descriptions and samples of process portfolios were presented. Preservice teachers who want to create a portfolio can use this chapter as a guide. Teacher education faculty may wish to use these guidelines to create a portfolio design for their students.

CHAPTER ACTIVITIES

1. Determine three or four program goals for a preservice teacher and describe the "products" that might be included in a portfolio to show how those goals were met.
2. Choose three INTASC standards. Analyze your teaching or classroom. Decide on ways in which you meet each of the standards chosen. Write a short description of why and how that specific INTASC standard is met. Include an overview of any evidence that helps you meet that standard.
3. If you knew your portfolio was going to be assessed either in an interview or presentation, which pieces of evidence would you want to be sure that you shared? Why?

WEB SITES

INTASC portfolio development
http://www.ccsso.org/projects/

Penn State's Center for Excellence in Teaching and Learning (portfolio development Web site)
http://www.psu.edu/celt/portfolio.html

REFERENCES

Barton, J., & Collins, A. (1993). Portfolios in teacher education. *Journal of Teacher Education, 44*(33), 200–209.

Campbell, D. M., Cignetti, P. B., Melenyzer, B. J., Nettles, D. H., & Wyman, R. M., Jr. (1997). *How to develop a professional portfolio: A manual for teachers.* Boston: Allyn & Bacon.

Interstate New Teacher Assessment and Support Consortium. (1992). *Model standards for beginning teacher licensing and development: A resource for state dialogue.* Washington, DC: Council of Chief State School Officers.

CHAPTER 5

Getting a Job

Many teachers use a portfolio to help secure a teaching position. In metropolitan areas where jobs are competitive, the portfolio can be the ticket a teacher needs to get a desirable position. The "job portfolio" is different from those created at other stages of a teaching career because it is created specifically for an external audience, one that will make a career decision based on its contents and other criteria. The portfolio is taken on a job interview at the district office or school level. Hurst and Wilson (1998) state that the number of success stories of teaching candidates who use portfolios to secure positions multiplies each year. The marketability of potential candidates has changed in the last 15 years due to the influx of technology. Vitas, portfolios, and Web pages have become more of the norm rather than the exception when searching for a desirable position.

Sample Product Portfolio Set Up by Responsibilities

Teaching Second Grade:
Sample units, classroom activities, strategies, classroom management plan, sample student work for this grade level

Contributing to School:
Work on previous committees, grade levels, or collaboration with other teachers

Professional Development:
Certificates from conferences attended, development plan, memberships in professional organizations

Danielson (1996) states, "When a teacher wants to move to a professionally more rewarding or more challenging position, the teacher must document excellence." One way to do this is through the portfolio. Portfolios are vivid visual representations of a teacher. Most would agree that interviews alone are inadequate for communicating the full range of a teacher's abilities. Used as a supplement in a job interview, the portfolio can provide evidence of a teacher's knowledge, skills, and disposition about education. Cook and Kessler (1993) assert that the portfolio can be used as a tool, which in addition to a teacher's credentials will allow the candidate to market him- or herself effectively. Portfolios allow teachers to show who they are and what they believe through concrete evidence.

THE OPTIONS

There are two types of portfolios that are appropriate to use when searching for a job—product and showcase portfolios (see Chapter 2 for more information). Prospective teachers will decide which of these to use based on their knowledge of the position desired. If one knows the grade level, school, educational philosophy, and other information about the school, then a product portfolio can be created. It would contain evidence that demonstrates a person's specific knowledge, skills, and abilities related to specific job responsibilities. Evidence would be chosen with the job qualifications in mind. Categories would be determined by job responsibilities. For each category, there would be a reflection. In these reflections, the teacher would talk about how each category relates to the specific job and how the evidence shows his or her qualifications for the position. In other words, each reflection would show the candidate's ability to do the job well.

While the product portfolio is an excellent choice, most prospective teachers don't know in which grade level or even which school they will interview. Therefore, a showcase portfolio might be a better choice. Remember, in a showcase portfolio, developers choose the work best showing their abilities, knowledge, and dispositions. This type of portfolio can be organized by standards or domains (see Chapters 2, 4, and 7). Under each standard or domain, a developer would place "best" works. The reflection for each standard or domain would show a candidate's knowledge, abilities, and disposition. Frameworks discussed in Chapter 7 can be used to set up a job-seeking portfolio. Those candidates wanting a technology-driven product should review Chapter 8.

Sample Showcase Portfolio
High School Science Position

Teaching Beliefs:
Written statement of teaching philosophy

Teaching:
Excellent biology unit, lab lesson plans, and write-ups; lesson plans showing differentiated assignments

Classroom Management:
Classroom rules, diagram of classroom, motivation strategies

Professional Development:
Goals for the future, professional conferences attended, memberships in professional organizations

THINGS TO INCLUDE

There are some things that should be included in all portfolios used for job searches. To find out the answer to this, the potential audience for this portfolio—principals and personnel directors—were contacted by the authors. Our survey found that principals and teachers on interview teams at the school level were more interested in reviewing the portfolio than were the administrators at central offices. We also found that the portfolio can "break a tie" between two candidates who seem equal. Cole (1991) found that portfolios give teacher candidates a competitive edge over other candidates with equal credentials. Finally, the principals and personnel directors said that there were a few things that were mandatory in the portfolio:

1. Put the portfolio in a three-ring binder so it's easy to view.
2. Have an attractive, colorful cover sheet that includes the developer's name and licensure area(s).
3. Include a table of contents showing domains or sections so it is user friendly.
4. Include sample lesson plans and units. Student learning should be the main consideration when compiling the portfolio.
5. Include a beliefs statement or teaching philosophy.
6. Include a resume.
7. Don't misspell any words.
8. Make it neat, attractive, and manageable—don't include every piece of evidence collected over the last 6 years. Be selective.

Figures 5–1, 5–2, and 5–3 provide examples of portfolio evidence.

Mandatory Evidence

1. Three-ring binder
2. Attractive cover sheet
3. Table of contents
4. Lesson plans
5. Beliefs statement
6. Resume
7. No misspelled words
8. Neat work
9. Manageable evidence

Careful consideration of contents and creative displays will add value to a job portfolio. It is important to review the essential components of a portfolio presented in Chapter 2 (purpose, audience, evidence, and reflections). If a candidate is preparing a portfolio for job interviewing or promotion only, the "less is better" adage should be adhered to by the teacher. A cumbersome, thick portfolio may not be appealing to potential principals or interview teams.

Portfolio

Elizabeth K. Smith

Spring Semester, 2000
East Forks Elementary

FIGURE 5–1   Sample Cover Sheet

Table of Contents

Introductory Information

- Resume
- Philosophy of education
- Transcript

Unit Plan

Classroom Management Plan

Professional Evaluations

- Letters
- Teaching observations
- Teacher licensure

FIGURE 5–2   Sample Table of Contents

Resume for Susan Thomas

Susan Thomas
2158 Pleasing Place
Monroe, NC 28111

Education:

Bachelor of Science Degree, 2000
East Carolina University
K–6 Education

1995 Honor Graduate
Smithfield-Selma High School
Smithfield, North Carolina

Work Experience:

January–December 1999
Internship in Kindergarten Classroom
Stocks Elementary School
Tarboro, North Carolina
Contact Person: Ms. Tonya Perkins
Phone: (252) 555-1212

September 1998–May 1999
Clerical Worker and Receptionist
Student Advisement Center
Education Department
East Carolina University
Contact Person: Mrs. Polly Johnson
Phone: (252) 555-1212

February 1997–September 1998
Sales Clerk and Wedding Consultant
Reading China and More
Greenville, North Carolina
No longer in business

FIGURE 5–3   Sample Resume

January 1996–February 1997
Waitress
Annabelle's Restaurant
Greenville, North Carolina
No longer in business

Summer of 1996
Sales Clerk
Royal Doulton China
Smithfield, North Carolina

Summer of 1994, 1995
Lifeguard and Swimming Instructor
Smithfield Family Pool
Contact Person: Mr. Tommy Austin
252-555-1111

References:

Ms. Tonya Perkins
Principal
3710 Cancion Street
Tarboro Elementary School
Rocky Mount, NC 26858
252-555-1212

Mrs. Ethel Warner
University Supervisor
1000 College Lane
Greenville, NC 27858
252-555-1212

Mrs. Polly Perkins
Work Supervisor
Annabelle's Restaurant
Greenville, NC 27858
252-555-1212

E-mail me! Stmail@mailprogram.net

FIGURE 5–3   Sample Resume—*continued*

Sample Evidence for Job Portfolios

Table of contents—showing sections or organization
Resume—placed in front
Samples of student work—related to unit of study
Statement of philosophy—a short statement documenting what a teacher
    believes about students and learning
Official documents—certifications, test scores
Personal goals—things a teacher wants to achieve in his or her career
Personal data—placed at the beginning, optional
Autobiography—a self-reflection that will help readers understand
    the teacher
Letters of recommendation—from cooperating teachers and professors
Evaluations—from outside, although student teaching evaluations are fine
Photographs and visual documentation—related to the curriculum or other
    classroom activities
Goals for the students of tomorrow—a vision statement for a teacher's
    future classroom
Student and parent sentiments—notes, cards, or other positive feedback
Samples of college work—papers or projects related to teaching
Thematic units—units of study for students, the *most valuable evidence*
Learning activities—good, student-centered techniques that have been tried
Original ideas—anything spectacular and inventive for the classroom
Examples of students' work—related to the unit or the lessons included
    in the portfolio
Reflections—for each piece of evidence
Inspirational items—poems, sayings, pictures, or mottos that have an
    impact on teaching

THE JOB INTERVIEW

The portfolio should be taken to all job interviews, including those at the central office and school level. Inform interviewers of the portfolio, but don't push it on them. Most principals and teachers will review it. Usually, a principal will review it for 10 minutes, while an interview team of teachers will allot approximately 30 minutes. Another choice will be for the teacher to use it to answer interview questions. For example, when asked what type of teaching strategies were used, open the portfolio and point out several lessons that incorporate different techniques. This behavior will demonstrate a teacher's ability to "talk the talk and walk the walk." A word of caution for this suggestion: A teacher must know the portfolio well in order to do this. During a 30-minute interview, it doesn't look good to fumble through a portfolio looking for something. Another choice would be to leave the portfolio for a day so it can be reviewed.

CLOSING THOUGHTS

Portfolios are useful when interviewing for a job. The evidence allows the teacher to show his or her knowledge, skills, and abilities. Teachers who create portfolios for this purpose are viewed as organized and productive. Those who interview potential teachers view the portfolio as a way to see who best meets the qualifications for the job and who will be successful in a particular school or district. Finally, the portfolio gives credence to a teacher's beliefs and actions. This credence can get a teacher the job he or she desires.

CHAPTER ACTIVITIES

Pretend you are applying for a job. Determine the type of portfolio that would be most beneficial for you to share with the interviewer, and explain why. Describe various types of evidence you would include in that portfolio and explain why you included them. Classify the evidence into categories according to the job description and determine how and why the evidence would help you get the job.

REFERENCES

Cole, D., et al. (1991). Developing reflection in educational course work via the professional portfolio. *GATEways to Teacher Education, 4*, 10.

Cook, D., & Kessler, J. (1994) The professional teaching portfolio: A useful tool for an effective job search. 1994 *ASCUS Annual*, 15.

Danielson, C. (1996). *Enhancing professional practice: A framework for teaching.* Alexandria, VA: Association for Supervision and Curriculum Development.

Hurst, B., & Wilson, C. (1998). Professional teaching portfolios. *Phi Delta Kappan, 79*, 578–583.

CHAPTER 6

Portfolios for Continuing Licensure

Each year, at all stages of their careers, teachers are evaluated by their principals. In most cases, there is a preconference, an observation by the principal, and a postconference. During the observation, some set of "approved criteria" is used, and during the postconference both strengths and weaknesses are reported to the teacher. Often praise and suggestions for improvement are given to the teacher during the postconference. The active participant in this process is the principal who observes a teacher interacting with students and makes a judgment about his or her ability to teach effectively. The teacher usually assumes a reactionary role in the postconference—listening and responding. Evaluations performed in this matter are done "to the teacher" not "with the teacher," because the teacher has no voice in the development of the evaluation. They can only react to what is written (Glatthorn, 1998b).

The use of teaching portfolios as an alternative form for continuing licensure and practicing teachers is becoming an acceptable method in school districts across the nation (Wolf, Lichtenstein, & Stevenson, 1997). Professionals recognize the complexity of teaching. The traditional teacher observation tools used for evaluation do not capture the 3,000 daily decisions made by teachers (Danielson, 2002). Portfolios as an alternative method allow teachers to have an active voice in their evaluation and use the results as a professional development tool. The process of developing a portfolio empowers teachers by involving them in their own evaluation. This can result in teachers having a sense of control as they use their portfolios to gain a new perspective on their teaching, to promote self-assessment and reflection, to investigate effective practices, and to enhance student learning and their own professional growth (Hunter, 1998). Specific information on preparing a portfolio is presented in Chapter 2 of this book.

PORTFOLIOS FOR NOVICE TEACHERS

As in other professions, it is the responsibility of teachers to demonstrate in their portfolios essential teaching competence using the standards developed and approved by their local school systems or states. It is also their responsibility to demonstrate their requisite knowledge, skills, and attitudes for teaching. This section deals with the portfolio for evaluating beginning teachers. In some states or school systems, teachers create portfolios as beginning teachers, while in other states they create specific products for licensure. There is a difference between a portfolio and a product. The portfolio is a collection of items the teacher selects to demonstrate his or her competence as a teacher. The product is a collection of evidence prescribed by the agency that will assess it based on the standards and activities identified by the school system or state. For example, required evidence could be: a 15-minute video, 10 consecutive lesson plans, two assessment measures, three case studies to accompany activities related to instruction, and so forth.

STANDARDS

As discussed in Chapters 2 and 3, the standards on which beginning teachers frequently demonstrate their teaching competence are the INTASC standards, which were developed by the Interstate New Teacher Assessment and Support Consortium (INTASC). The audience for the licensing portfolio is the school system's licensure officer or board, or the state licensing board assessors. Regardless of who the licensing officials are, the purpose of the development of a beginning teacher's portfolio is to secure a continuing license based on standards.

 INTASC Standards

1. *Content Pedagogy*   The teacher understands the central concepts, tools of inquiry, and structures of the discipline he or she teaches and can create learning experiences that make these aspects of subject matter meaningful to students.

2. *Student Development*   The teacher understands how children learn and develop, and can provide opportunities that support a child's intellectual, social, and personal development.

INTASC Standards—continued

3. *Diverse Learners*   The teacher understands how children differ in their approaches to learning and creates instructional opportunities that are adapted to diverse learners.

4. *Multiple Instructional Strategies*   The teacher understands and uses a variety of instructional strategies to encourage student development of critical thinking, problem solving, and performance skills.

5. *Motivation and Management*   The teacher uses an understanding of individual and group motivation and behavior to create a learning environment that encourages positive social interaction, active engagement in learning, and self-motivation.

6. *Communication and Technology*   The teacher uses knowledge of effective verbal, nonverbal, and media communication techniques to foster active inquiry, collaboration, and supportive interaction in the classroom.

7. *Planning*   The teacher plans instruction based on knowledge of the subject matter, students, the community, and curriculum goals.

8. *Assessment*   The teacher understands and uses formal and informal assessment strategies to evaluate and ensure the continuous intellectual, social, and physical development of the learner.

9. *Reflective Practice: Professional Growth*   The teacher is a reflective practitioner who continually evaluates the efforts of his or her choices and actions on others (students, parents, and other professionals in the learning community) and who actively seeks out opportunities to grow professionally.

10. *School and Community Involvement*   The teacher fosters relationships with school colleagues, parents, and agencies in the larger community to support students' learning and well-being.

Sample Types of Evidence

- Unit and daily lesson plans
- Parent communications
- Videotapes
- Management plans
- Samples of student work
- Case studies
- Record of professional activities
- Teacher-made assessments
- Summative evaluations
- Pictures
- Parent, student, and peer surveys
- Log of parent contacts

COORDINATED SETS OF EVIDENCE

Novice teachers need to have evaluation criteria connected to their daily work. Whether a beginning teacher creates a portfolio or a product, evidence will probably be similar. For this section, we will focus on the performance-based product (PBP). Ideas and evidence presented in this section could easily be applied to a general portfolio if that is the requirement or option for a novice teacher. The PBP is a collection of evidence produced during the normal course of teaching. This process recognizes the very different contexts in which teachers work and provides them with the autonomy to present that which best reflects their knowledge and skill in that context. According to Wolf (1991), it is a means of "storing and displaying evidence of a teacher's knowledge and skills." The PBP, unlike more traditional means of assessment, can reflect the richness and complexity of teaching over extended periods of time. By selecting multiple sources of evidence in authentic settings and compiling it over time, teachers are able to focus and reflect on the products of their teaching and their students' learning. Novice teachers

The Portfolio Machine

developing a performance-based product are empowered to evaluate their progress and improve their skills. Evidence representing the beginning teacher's best work, with reflections, is gathered through a systematic process that ultimately is compiled into a finished product and submitted for licensure review. Because final products are usually limited in size and content, beginning teachers select the evidence that provides the most comprehensive picture possible.

Sample by Area Organization

- Demonstrating content knowledge and ability to teach
- Classroom management and its environment
- Professional responsibility
- Measurement of student learning

ORGANIZATION OF EVIDENCE

Beginning-teacher portfolios are organized around a coordinated set of evidence as prescribed by the employing system or state. The evidence may be presented standard by standard, for example, Standard 1, Standard 2, and so forth, or the organization may be presented by areas of teaching, such as management, curriculum, instruction, and assessment (see the previous box). Various activities may also be the organizing framework for the portfolio. An example of an activity is: "*Create a parent survey that gathers information about how parents perceive your effectiveness in his or her child's teacher. Randomly choose five parents to complete the survey. Summarize the survey findings.*"

In both of the last two organizational structures, the standards and the specific indicators are identified in the area or activity. Figures 6–1 and 6–2 are sample surveys.

REFLECTION

Cycle of Reflections for a Continuing Licensure Portfolio

Whether a beginning teacher is creating a product or a portfolio, the reflection cycle is the same as outlined in Chapter 3. In a portfolio, a reflection is created for each piece of evidence. For a product that has coordinated sets of evidence, a reflection is written for each set of evidence. A set of evidence may include one lesson or five lesson plans, plus student work, depending on the criteria for the product. For each reflection, the candidate will describe, analyze, and finally plan, as outlined in Chapter 3 of this book.

Parent/Guardian Survey

Teacher's Name: _____

Thank you for your help. The information from this survey will be invaluable to your child's teacher. Please check the following items that describe your experience with the teacher. No individual parents will be identified with these survey forms.

Have you asked for:

	Yes	No
1. An overview of class content and goals?	____	____
2. A description of your child's progress?	____	____
3. Ideas for home support of learning?	____	____

Has the teacher provided you with:

	Yes	No
4. An overview of class content and goals?	____	____
5. A description of your child's progress?	____	____
6. Ideas for home support of learning?	____	____

Circle the number that best describes your opinion.

	Yes				No	Don't Know
7. Did your child seem to know what was expected of him or her in this class?	5	4	3	2	1	0
8. Did the classroom work seem to be the right challenge, not too hard or too easy?	5	4	3	2	1	0
9. Were you satisfied with your child's overall classroom experience as provided by this teacher?	5	4	3	2	1	0

Additional comments:

_____

_____

_____

_____

Please add any additional comments on the back of this form.

FIGURE 6–1 Sample

Parent/Guardian Survey

NAME: _____

RELATIONSHIP TO CHILD: _____

NOTE TO PARENT: Please complete and place this survey in the envelope provided.

	strongly disagree				strongly agree
1. *My child is treated fairly by this teacher.*	1	2	3	4	5
Comments:					
2. *I know the expectations this teacher has for my child.*	1	2	3	4	5
Comments:					
3. *My child likes to attend this teacher's class.*	1	2	3	4	5
Comments:					

4. *My child's teacher has kept me informed about my child's progress.*
   Comments:

5. *My child's teacher keeps me informed through:*

Please check all that apply:
_____ phone calls _____ progress reports _____ home visits
_____ letter or memo _____ school conferences _____ other [please specify]

6. *My child's teacher contacts me:*
Please check only one:
_____ daily   _____ once a week   _____ once a month   _____ never
                      _____ several times   _____ several times a month
                      each week   _____ as often as needed

7. *Describe any changes in your child's attitude toward learning or toward school that you can credit to this teacher.*

8. *Do you feel that your child is learning in this teacher's classroom? Why or why not?*

Please add any additional comments on the back of this form.

FIGURE 6–2 Sample

Connections to Make Between Evidences and Reflection

Reflection is the keystone to the performance-based product. It is critical to the novice teacher's development. Through reflection, the teacher begins the ongoing process of blending the art and science of effective teaching practice. Reflections require thoughtful and careful reporting and analysis of teaching practice, philosophy, and experience. Understanding why an activity or practice was productive or nonproductive in the classroom is a key element in the progression from novice teacher to master teacher (Dietz, 1995; Sparks, 1997). The reflection process is the glue that connects each coordinated set of evidence to standards. Therefore, it is important for a novice teacher to connect to each standard that he or she is meeting or required to meet during the reflection process.

The reflections are also vital to the person or persons responsible for judging whether the teacher has met the required level of performance for each standard or activity. The reflections allow the teacher to learn from their experiences and determine where they have been and where they want to go next.

> **Note:**   Review Chapter 3 to refresh yourself on the purpose and construction of reflections.

Examples of Reflections

The reflections included in a performance-based product developed by a beginning teacher focus not only on the activity or area required by the school system or state, but also on the connection between the evidence and the established standards. By explaining how the evidence addresses standards through the activity or area, the reflection helps the beginning teacher put evidence into perspective for the assessors. In the case of the INTASC standards, and most standards, the indicators for each are important and must be addressed in the reflection. The examples below show reflections that address standards and indicators.

First Example

Nancy Lilley,* a non-Hispanic White woman, was a first-semester senior during her field experience in a rural, low-socioeconomic school. Her class, seventh-grade physical science, was composed of students identified as slow learners. Nancy had been present in these students' classroom 1 day a week for the past month. She had observed the students and provided them with one-on-one assistance on her previous days.

*Not her real name

DESCRIBE

I taught a lesson on March 30 at 9:30 a.m. that met five of the INTASC standards. The lesson met Standard 1, exhibiting content knowledge, because I displayed an understanding of the content and effectively transferred that information to the students. It met Standard 2, student development, because I provided for students' various learning styles by using manipulatives, writing exercises, and oral communication. Because of the group's diversity, I provided a variety of experiences, meeting Standard 3, accommodating diverse learners. The lesson met Standard 4, using multiple teaching strategies, because I used strategies to encourage thinking on different levels by expecting my students to make connections while I stated the obvious. Last, I incorporated Standard 5, demonstrating management and motivation, because I was aware of the important social interaction with this class and used it to create a more positive environment for learning.

The class was seventh-grade boys and girls, the majority of whom were African-American males. Most were repeating the grade and had barely passed the sixth-grade competency test. The class was a lively group and not well disciplined, but I took that into consideration when planning the format I used to teach the lesson.

The lesson focused on simple machines. I began by having the students write a few notes about what they knew about simple machines. Then we brainstormed together about things we see everyday that might be simple machines. Everyone was involved in the discussion. Next, I spent 15 minutes describing each of the six simple machines and demonstrating with models I had brought with me. The students were able to watch, reflect, and then work with the models. We discussed as a large group, worked in small groups that I supervised, and reflected individually about what we saw, touched, and wrote. In addition, I encouraged vocabulary building and note taking using a handout we completed together. During the remaining time, the students worked on hidden word puzzles I had created for the lesson.

Analysis

I used the textbook as the lesson's foundation, but I constructed my own teaching props. There was a great deal of interest because of the immediacy of the subject matter. The lesson was the most successful I had taught these students (it was my third). My students were even able to reduce some complicated machines to simple terms. Science helped them explain their world. It showed them that science is useful, and it is valuable because it was not clear enough to be useful as a reinforcement tool. I had to do more explaining than I planned or wanted to do. The class was not quiet, but for the most part the students all stayed on task. The lesson probably included a little more information than could be efficiently mastered in one class period. The introduction of simple machines alone, without definitions and equations, would have been enough. All in all, the lesson was a positive experience for my students and for me.

Future Impact

This teaching episode showed me the value of making academic information relevant and real. For a socially active class like this one, a lesson like this, which lent itself to group interaction, was positive. I was well prepared and the students were interested, which meant that maintaining discipline was easier. It showed me that it is necessary to acknowledge where these students are and what they are interested in. The lesson reinforced the importance of preparation, appropriate teaching strategies, and my students' needs.

Author's Reaction

Nancy Lilley wrote an informative reflection for a beginning teacher. Her analysis is consistent with the concerns of beginning teachers. A strength of the reflection is the linking of the INTASC standards to her teaching experience. An area to improve on is the Future Impact section. It could have more detail and correlation with issues discussed in the description and analysis sections. It is important for a teacher to be focused when writing reflections that correlate with standards.

Second Example

There are also reflections that focus on one or more pieces of related evidence. The following reflection is an example.

Jack Morino* is a second-year teacher in a small city. He teaches a fourth-grade elementary class of children from low- and middle-income homes. The pieces of evidence for this reflection are two floor plans of the classroom, before and after, and the accompanying seating charts.

*Not his real name.

INTASC standards met by this evidence:
 2. *Student development*
 5. *Motivation*

   Much time is spent moving about the classroom, handing things in, going to centers, picking up corrected work, and working on projects and activities. I have set up my classroom so that students can get to these places more efficiently without wasting time or steps. I have analyzed my classroom environment and made adjustments, such as moving mailboxes to the front of the room from the rear, thus saving time and steps. Desks are arranged in groups so that all can see the front board. At times I place the morning assignments and activities on the front board, giving students some choice of what order in which to complete them. This gives the students choice and helps them manage their time. It also helps them assume responsibility for their own work completion. Examples of classroom arrangements and board assignments can be seen on my video at time mark 00:09.

   Students like having the classroom set up to better meet their needs. I listen to students' concerns and try to physically arrange the room to make them comfortable. I have found that if they are too crowded they are not able to concentrate.

   I have learned that I have more time to teach and have students engaged in activities if I cut down on the time it takes to do little things like hand out papers and move around the room. This and my students' suggestions are what caused me to analyze my room arrangement and my paper procedures.

ASSESSMENT

The assessment of performance-based products involves scoring rubrics to evaluate each activity or area. In education assessment, a *rubric* is defined as a scoring guide that indicates the criteria to be used and several levels of performance

(Glatthorn, 1998a). The most frequently used types of rubric are the holistic and analytical. The **holistic rubric** usually has competency labels associated with it. The following box is an example of a rubric used to assess Planning for Instruction. It contains three competency labels: skillful, promising, and ineffective. However, only one score is given for the entire product. That is why it is called a holistic rubric. The **analytical rubric** uses the same set of competency labels for each category. The rubric is applied across different categories, for example, Instruction, Motivation, and Professional Growth, and a rating is given for each category (Linn & Gronlund, 1995). The analytical rubric is more useful for providing diagnostic feedback because it assesses individual categories, enabling a teacher to focus on the specific area where he or she received high or low ratings. Holistic rubrics, however, tend to be the rubrics that are used to assess performance-based products in the licensure process. This is because the purpose of the licensure process is to make a decision to "yes, issue a license to practice" or "no, do not issue a license to practice." It is summative in nature, and as such does not demand specific feedback or ratings by categories.

Sample Criteria

The Skillful Teacher's planned instructional strategies are designed to regularly engage students and encourage critical thought. This teacher often makes connections between the content being presented, the larger unit of study, and the students' daily lives. Materials and manipulatives are used to complement learning.

The Promising Teacher's planned instructional strategies do not always engage students, but alternately bore or frustrate them. The teacher does not always make connections between the lesson, the rest of the unit, and the students' daily realities. Materials and manipulatives are sometimes used to complement learning.

The Ineffective Teacher relies solely on lecture, worksheets, or workbooks, rarely planning to engage or challenge the students. This teacher does not make connections between lessons, the greater unit of study, or the students' daily lives. Materials are frequently outdated, inappropriate, or not used at all.
(From Teach for America's PAI document, 1996)

Criteria for performance-based products revolves around the standards that must be met. The language of the standards is developed into a holistic or analytical trait rubric based on the objectives or outcomes for each coordinated set of evidence. To the right is a holistic rubric for instruction. In the appendixes of this book are other examples of criteria-based rubrics.

STATE PERFORMANCE–BASED ASSESSMENT SYSTEMS

There are a number of states considering or developing performance-based processes for awarding continuing licenses to beginning teachers. Georgia, Florida, Oregon, Washington, New York, Connecticut, and North Carolina are in various stages of development. Each state has approached the process from a different perspective. Connecticut is generating performance-based guidelines for each discipline and is using the various learned society standards to guide the product and its assessment (e.g., the National Council of Teachers of Mathematics). On the other hand, North Carolina has developed the same performance-based product for all teaching areas and is using the INTASC standards for all.

One example of the organization of a performance-based product is to divide it into five areas, with each area addressing one or more of the INTASC standards. The five possible areas could be (1) content knowledge and how to teach it, (2) the learner and his or her unique needs, (3) classroom climate, (4) the school community link, and (5) evaluation of self as a professional. There would be required components for each area. For example, consider the area of Classroom Climate, which would address INTASC Standard 5. The required components for this area would be:

- A classroom management plan
- Comparison of discipline occurrences at the beginning and end of the year
- Video to support this area of contact with parents (e.g., a discipline log)
- Reflection

Developers would also include additional evidence to document this area and the related INTASC standard. Figure 6–3 is an outline of a classroom management plan.

Another organizational example using the INTASC standards is to set up a notebook (the product) and divide it into the 10 standards. The developers would then place pieces of evidence, or artifacts, into each standard and write a reflection on each artifact or on the standard as a whole. Some pieces of evidence would have a "value added" effect; that is, it would be applicable to more than one standard. An excellent example of a "value added" artifact is a contiguous set of lessons. It could be evidence in INTASC Standards 1, 2, 4, 6, 7 or 8. At the end of this organizational example would be a reflection on the evidence and the product as a whole.

A management plan is a must for any teacher who wishes to have a classroom that runs smoothly. It is an individual set of procedures and guidelines that reflect what a teacher believes about interacting with young people. The management plan must be developed within the policies and procedure already established by a school system and/or an individual school. This outline is a guide to assist teachers in developing a management plan.

I. **Identify the classroom rules.**
Remember to get student input and to include the rule, "Follow all school rules."

II. **Identify consequences for breaking or following the rules.**
The consequences may be different for each rule, or they may be an accumulation of rule violations or successes.

III. **Develop lesson plans to teach the rules and consequences.**
The most important concept a teacher will teach all year is appropriate behavior in the classroom so it can operate in an efficient and effective manner. Remember that students come from different cultures and backgrounds; thus, the class must discuss some words, phrases, and behaviors to come to a common understanding. This part of your plan should include parent/guardian notification.

IV. **Decide how you will assess whether or not students understand the rules and consequences.**
This and the teaching of the rules, consequences, and procedures is an ongoing effort. Update and review with the students on a regular basis.

V. **Establish the rules and consequences in the classroom.**
Remember what students want most from their teacher is to be treated fairly and with consistency.

FIGURE 6–3 Outline of Classroom Management Plan

INTRODUCTORY INFORMATION TO THE PERFORMANCE PRODUCT

No matter what organizational pattern the product takes, there is some information that must be gathered for placement at the beginning of the performance-based product.

- First, a biographical data sheet, which includes information about the beginning teacher and the college or university from which her or his degree was received.
- Second, demographic data regarding the school setting and the particular demographics of the beginning teacher's classroom (see Figure 6–4).
- Third, a signature sheet that has the signatures of the beginning teacher, the mentor, and the principal. This is designed to verify that the product has been completed by the teacher who is submitting the product.
- Fourth, a checklist to assist beginning teachers in their organization of the product (see Figure 6–5).

Candidate Name: _____ Candidate ID# _____ Soc. Sec. # _____
School: _____ District: _____
Grade(s): _____ Subject(s): _____

Please use a **BLACK PEN** and **CIRCLE** or **PRINT** your responses in the space provided. Unless otherwise indicated, check only one response for each question. Please respond to all questions.

1. Which of the following best describes the **LEVEL** of the class being observed?

   a. Pre-Kindergarten–Grade 2
   b. Grades 3–5
   c. Grades 6–8
   d. Grades 9–12
   e. More than one of the levels above
      (please specify) _____

2. Which of the following best describes the **CONTENT** of the class being observed?

   a. Business
   b. Computer science
   c. English as a second language
   d. Foreign language
   e. Health/physical education
   f. Home economics
   g. Language arts/communications
   h. Mathematics
   i. Physical/biological/chemical sciences
   j. Social sciences
   k. Special education
   l. Visual arts/ music/theater/dance
   m. Vocational education
   n. Other (please specify) _____

3. Which of the following best describes the areas from which your students come? (Check **ALL** that apply.)

   a. Low income, urban
   b. Middle or upper income, urban
   c. Low income, suburban
   d. Middle or upper income, suburban
   e. Low income, small town (not suburban)
   f. Middle or upper income, small town (not suburban)
   g. Low income, rural
   h. Middle or upper income, rural

4. [   ] What is the **TOTAL NUMBER** of students enrolled in the class to be observed?

5. [   ] a. What is the number of **MALE** students?
       b. What is the number of **FEMALE** Students?

6. [   ] What is the **AGE** range for all of the students in the class?

7. What is the estimated number of students identified in each **RACIAL/ETHNIC GROUP**?

   [   ] a. African American or Black
   [   ] b. Asian American/Asian (Ex.: Japanese, Chinese, Korean)
   [   ] c. Pacific Island American/Pacific Islander
   [   ] d. Mexican, Mexican American, or Chicano
   [   ] e. Other Hispanic, Latino, or Latin American
   [   ] f. Native American, American Indian, or Alaskan Native
   [   ] g. White
   [   ] h. Other (please specify)

8. What is the estimated number of students in each of the following **LANGUAGE** categories?

   [   ] a. English language proficient
   [   ] b. Limited English language proficient

9. Approximately what **PERCENTAGE** of your class can be categorized as the following?

   (Percentage)
   [   ] a. Above-average or advanced skill level
   [   ] b. Average or intermediate skill level
   [   ] c. Below-average skill level
   100% Total

10. Approximately how many students in this class have been identified as having **EXCEPTIONALITIES**?

   [   ] a. Blind or visually impaired
   [   ] b. Deaf or hearing impaired
   [   ] c. Developmentally disabled
   [   ] d. Emotionally or behaviorally disabled
   [   ] e. Gifted
   [   ] f. Learning disabled
   [   ] g. Physically disabled
   [   ] h. Other (please specify)

Adapted from Praxis III, Educational Testing Service

FIGURE 6–4   Sample Class Profile

Checklist

Please complete this checklist to ensure that you have included everything necessary for an assessor to accurately evaluate your Performance-Based Product. **Be sure that all information is contained in your notebook, including your video.**

_____ **Biographical Data Sheet**
_____ **Signature Sheet**
_____ **Class Profile**
_____ **Videotape (no longer than 30 minutes total)**

Category One - Planning and Instruction
_____ Unit plans and goals
_____ Five contiguous lesson plans
_____ Related student work and test/assessment data
_____ Student achievement log
_____ Evidence/artifacts
_____ Video
_____ Video information sheet
_____ Reflection

Category Two - School and Community
_____ Professional contribution log
_____ Contact log
_____ Parent survey(s) and summary
_____ Evidence/artifacts
_____ Reflection

Category Three - Management and Motivation
_____ Classroom management plan
_____ Comparison of discipline rates
_____ Evidence/artifacts
_____ Video
_____ Video information sheet
_____ Reflection

Category Four - Understanding the Learner
_____ Case Studies
_____ Related student work and test/assessment data
_____ Evidence/artifacts
_____ Video
_____ Video information sheet
_____ Reflection

Category Five - Professional Growth
_____ Beginning Teacher Individual Growth Plan (for all years)
_____ Self-administered interview for year 1
_____ Self-administered interview for year 2
_____ Self-administered interview for year 3 (if applicable)
_____ Summative evaluation for year 1
_____ Summative evaluation for year 2
_____ Summative evaluation for year 3 (if applicable)
_____ Reflection

FIGURE 6–5   Sample Performance-Based Product Checklist

Following these information sheets are areas or standards with the evidence to support them.

In Appendix B are samples of how North Carolina and Connecticut are implementing performance-based products, using the INTASC standards, for all beginning teachers. These have been chosen for inclusion because they appear to be the most developed, are highly reliable, and have been implemented statewide (Jaeger & Wrightman, 1999).

PORTFOLIOS FOR ALTERNATIVE FORMS OF EVALUATION OR LICENSURE RENEWAL

For the most part, teachers who develop portfolios once they have taught for 4 or more years do it for their professional growth. Portfolios created as an alternative to traditional teacher evaluation have two distinct purposes: (1) for teachers to show competence and (2) for teachers to grow professionally. The audience is the principal or immediate supervisor of the teacher, such as a department chairperson. The opportunity to develop a portfolio as a continuing teacher is reserved for the tenured teacher.

Teachers and administrators choose to implement professional portfolios for several reasons:

1. Portfolios are an alternative to traditional forms of assessment, thus allowing teachers more of a voice in their evaluation. Some teachers develop portfolios in addition to using traditional assessments, which can also be a positive experience for teachers because this can blend several types of "data" regarding their teaching.
2. Through the process of developing a portfolio, teachers become more reflective about their practice because the process of development requires a teacher to contemplate his/her own abilities.
3. A collaborative relationship can be developed between the teacher and administrator.
4. This type of portfolio development can be a precursor to developing a National Board portfolio (Hunter, 1998).

Another reason teachers should develop a portfolio is to provide documentation about their professional life. Components of the portfolio can also be used when applying for teaching awards or leadership positions.

OPTIONS FOR ORGANIZATION

Teaching portfolios developed by continuing teachers can have many different designs. There are two suggested frameworks for teachers and a different framework for other educators developing a professional portfolio for evaluation purposes. The first two frameworks for teachers are (1) by categories of teaching skills and abilities and (2) by categories of professional goals. Next, a framework for other educators is presented using categories of job responsibilities. Educators looking for cutting-edge options may choose to review Chapter 8 of this book, which discusses electronic portfolios. Any of the frameworks presented in this chapter can be used in an electronic design. Logistics for design in this chapter focus on the time line teachers use to develop portfolios. Options are for portfolios to be done (or redone) each year by teachers or developed using a "cycle" over several years. Continuing teachers can develop product, process, or showcase portfolios, but showcase is the most popular type, with product portfolios being the second choice. (See Chapter 2 for more information on portfolio types.)

Option for Organization: Teaching Skills and Abilities

A portfolio developed according to teaching skills and abilities has as its categories different areas of teaching and related activities (nonteaching duties such as committee work). The first framework (described in the following section) has its first four categories related to a district's evaluation instrument categories (found on most teacher evaluation instruments). The last category, other school involvement, relates to a separate criterion on many district evaluation instruments—nonteaching duties such as committee involvement, leadership opportunities, and other types of service to the school and district. The advantage of this design is that the categories give teachers a specific plan to follow, especially if it correlates to an evaluation instrument used by their principals. The first organizational framework to show teaching skills and abilities follows below.

Framework 1: District Evaluation Instrument Criteria by Categories

1. Discipline, teaching methods and strategies—focuses on content, units, and lessons taught and teaching and learning strategies.
2. Class environment—focuses on organization and structure of the classroom.
3. Preparation and organization—focuses on planning instruction.
4. Student evaluation—focuses on student assessment.
5. Other school involvement—focuses on other responsibilities carried out by a teacher.

In a portfolio divided by Framework 1 domains, a developer would place evidence in each of the categories to show competence in these areas. If a teacher wanted to create a showcase portfolio using this design, best work related to all of the categories would be included.

Framework 2: A Two-Domain Model

Another framework to show teaching skills and abilities has fewer categories, something that could be the choice of the developer.

This option allows teachers to demonstrate their knowledge, abilities, and dispositions using a two-domain design. Think about the two main responsibilities of a teacher: teaching and classroom management. This design highlights these areas. Category 1 is Teaching and Assessing Students, which is broad enough to include all elements related to teaching. The second category is Classroom Climate, which includes management, motivation, and communication. These categories also correlate with propositions of the National Board for Professional Teaching Standards (NBPTS). The advantage of this design is its simplicity. Since many teaching tasks are interrelated, the breadth of Category 1 allows teachers to include a variety of evidence that would overlap. Category 2 gives teachers the opportunity to specifically document their efforts toward classroom management and student motivation. Teachers could develop showcase or product portfolios using this design as well.

Framework 2 Example

Category 1: Teaching and Assessing Students—focuses on content knowledge, meeting diverse students' needs, strategies, planning, and formal and informal assessment.

NBPTS Propositions: The teacher knows the subject he or she teaches and how to teach this subject to students. Teachers are committed to students and their learning.

Category 2: Classroom Climate—focuses on climate, communication, and student management.

NBPTS Proposition: Teachers are responsible for managing and monitoring student learning.

Framework 3: A Different Kind of Educator

Some teachers or personnel who work in schools don't have traditional teaching responsibilities. Librarians, teacher assistants, and counselors, to name a few, interact with students in a different way than do classroom teachers. Thus, traditional organizational formats that outline classroom teaching skills and abilities do not match the job responsibilities of certain school personnel. The process of organizing the portfolio would be the same for these professionals as for those set out for teachers outlined earlier in this chapter. A format for these related positions follows.

Category 1: Job Responsibilities—*focuses on specific responsibilities; may come from district or state guidelines.*

Category 2: Professional Development—*focuses on professional goals set by the professional.*

PROFESSIONAL GOALS: ANOTHER OPTION FOR ORGANIZATION

Each year teachers, schools, and districts set goals for themselves. Many teachers often create a yearly professional development plan that contains one to three goals set by them. Often teachers reflect school or district initiatives within their plan. Portfolios are then developed around the professional goals. Professional goals can be a category within a portfolio, or an entire portfolio can be organized around professional goals. The purpose of a professional goal portfolio is to promote self-learning and continue systematic reflection and growth for professional teachers, no matter how long they have taught. Portfolios created using this framework would follow product portfolio guidelines (see Chapter 2), with developers including evidence that demonstrates they met every professional goal.

Organization:
1. Give the professional goal.
2. Outline the goal, identifying how it will be met.
3. Include evidence that shows how each goal is met.
4. Write a reflection on the obtained goal.

Reflections

As discussed in Chapter 3, reflection is an essential component of portfolio development. Portfolios for continuing teachers also must contain reflections. For each teaching category, reflections should focus on why he or she is an effective teacher. Sample reflection questions include: What skills and knowledge am I demonstrating with this evidence? What category am I showing competence in (Planning, Classroom Management, etc.)? What are my strengths as a teacher? (See the sample reflection later in this chapter.)

Reflections should be written for each of the professional goals. Reflections should have several parts: What is the goal? What were the steps in meeting it? Was it met? How? What did the teacher learn from this goal? What was changed or implemented as a result of this goal? What are the "next steps" based on the goal?

Reflections are the defining element of a portfolio. The content and reflections of portfolios can be developed using several methods, discussed in the next section.

Logistics

Continuing teachers can develop a "new" portfolio each year or can develop a portfolio on a 2- or 3-year cycle. Using a process portfolio design, a 2- or 3-year cycle is set. The cycle works best for the professional goal category. During the 1st year, the teacher decides on two or three big goals and works on them over the entire cycle. At the end of the 1st year, progress toward the goals and, possibly, new goals building on these are reviewed and discussed. At the end of the cycle, a teacher's goal attainment is evaluated. For the next cycle, new goals are set. Another 2- or 3-year-cycle option that combines both purposes is as follows:

Year 1:   Teacher shows competency in teaching areas.
Year 2:   If competency is shown in year 1, professional goals are set during this year. At the end of the year, progress toward (or attainment of) professional goals is addressed. As previously discussed, new goals may be set that build on initial ones.
Year 3:   Evidence is collected to show goals. At the end of the 3-year cycle, attainment of goals is evaluated by the teacher, then usually the principal.

The next year, a new cycle begins with new goals.

ASSESSMENT OF THESE PORTFOLIOS

It is important to note that principals or other administrators may reserve the right to decide who will be required to compile a portfolio. If a teacher is deemed competent through traditional evaluation methods, he or she may be given the opportunity to use an alternative type of evaluation. Teachers who demonstrate competency in the classroom can receive different feedback than those who are working toward minimum competency. Thus, feedback may be more informal and should provide teachers with information to help them grow and reflect on their own abilities. Langer (1995) asserts that collaboration between professionals and vision about what a teacher's professional life should be like are two essential components for successful teaching portfolios.

Conferences

Teachers and administrators should have a collaborative conference to discuss the contents of the portfolio. Prior to the conference, administrators should have an opportunity to review and read the portfolio contents. The portfolio framework and categories should drive the conference discussion. Since the administrator is the primary audience for the portfolio, an evaluation using a rubric, checklist, or anecdotal record format may be used. A formal document showing pass or fail can be included. More helpful to the teacher is a written response outlining strengths, insights, and areas in which to improve or expand. The written feedback will benefit the teacher when selecting his or her next professional goals.

Sample Questions for Portfolio Interviews

1. What are your strengths in relation to teaching?
2. What are areas where you need to improve, in your opinion?
3. What other types of activities do you use in your classroom?
4. What are other types of assessments used in your classroom?
5. What is your next professional goal?
6. What have you learned from this experience?
7. How do your professional goals correlate with school? The district? Other goals?
8. What areas, related to instruction, do you feel are needed to make you a more effective teacher?

RUBRICS

Another method to judge portfolios is the use of rubrics. A rubric is a scoring guide that gives specific scoring criteria. A rubric may be used to evaluate whether or not a goal is met, or if teaching and assessing strategies are at an acceptable standard. While the portfolio is mainly for the teacher, the principal or supervisor will probably need to judge it against the standard. The rubric allows the principal to "evaluate" the portfolio against the predetermined purpose, thus holding the teacher accountable for the portfolio process.

PROCESS FOR USING SCORING EVALUATION CRITERIA

Since portfolios are authentic products, they are used more for self-analysis and reflection. The categories on the rubric are meant to guide discussion about the development of the portfolio for the next school year. Principals and teachers may decide to use one or both categories. At the preconference stage, a discussion should be held on the evaluation criteria for the rubric, with both parties having an opportunity to discuss their preferences. The developer will select goals for the portfolio.

At the postconference stage, the portfolio would be evaluated using the criteria. An area (at, above, or below) would be selected. Strengths and Areas to Improve/Future Goals will be filled out for each category. At this time, future goals and next steps can be addressed. One of the main objectives of this rubric is to promote an open dialogue between the teacher and administrator about the portfolio contents.

So far in this chapter, frameworks, reflections, and assessment have been discussed. Following are examples of portfolios developed by practicing educators using several of the frameworks outlined in this chapter.

Directions: For this general rubric, a teacher would receive a score for both Teaching Responsibilities and Professional Goals. This is just an example. Rubrics can be developed by the teacher and administrator; for other sample rubrics, see Danielson (2002).

Teacher: _____ Subjects Taught: _____

Date:

Level	Teaching Responsibilities	Professional Goals
Above standard	Evidence shows that this candidate has the knowledge, skills, and abilities to demonstrate he or she is above standard in relation to teaching responsibilities. Sample indicators: This teacher uses strategies and skills that are effective and student centered, assessments that match objectives, and strategies to manage and motivate students to be successful. Critical and other strategies are used with all students. Works well with parents and community.	Evidence shows that this candidate has met his or her professional goals in an exemplary way, demonstrated through evidence selected and reflections written. This goal is met and has an impact on students' learning in some way.
At standard	Evidence shows that this candidate has the knowledge, skills, and abilities to be at standard in relation to teaching responsibilities. Sample indicators: Teacher writes and delivers effective lesson plans. A variety of appropriate strategies are used. Classroom is managed appropriately. This teacher does a good job in all areas related to teaching.	The professional goal was met, as demonstrated through evidence and written reflections.
Needs improvement	Evidence shows that this candidate may be lacking in some knowledge, skills, or abilities related to teaching responsibilities listed in this column. Area: _____	The professional goal was not met completely. Portions or segments of the goal need to be further developed. Area: _____
Unacceptable	Evidence shows that this candidate is lacking in knowledge, skills, or abilities related to teaching responsibilities listed in this column. This teacher would not have the majority of skills to be effective in the classroom.	The goal was not met.

FIGURE 6–6 Sample Rubric

(continued)

Narrative Feedback		
Strengths		
Areas to improve		
Future goals		

_____   _____
Administrator's Signature/Date   Teacher's Signature/Date

Process for using scoring evaluation criteria:
1. Since portfolios are authentic products, they are used more for self-analysis and reflection. The categories on the rubric are meant to guide discussions about the development of the portfolio for the next school year. Principals and teachers may decide to use one or both categories. A discussion should be held at the preconference stage about the evaluation criteria for the rubric with both parties having an opportunity to discuss their preferences.
2. An area would be selected (at, above, needs improvement, unacceptable).
3. Strengths and Areas to improve/Future goals will be filled out for each category.
4. One of the main objectives of this rubric is to promote an open dialogue between the teacher and administrator about the portfolio contents.

FIGURE 6–6 *(Concluded)*

SAMPLES OF ALTERNATIVE EVALUATION PORTFOLIOS

Portfolio Sample 1

Carolyn Smith developed her first portfolio in her 29th year of teaching. She teaches third grade in a rural community school. As a tenured teacher, Carolyn chose to develop a showcase portfolio based on five given domains related to teaching. In the first year of a 3-year cycle, she demonstrated her teaching ability through her portfolio. In her classroom, she uses a unit-based approach arising from the research literature. Her goal is to use a variety of strategies that are hands-on, relevant to students' lives, and developmentally appropriate.

Purpose:
To demonstrate the knowledge, skills, and abilities of teaching; to take charge of her own professional development

Type of Portfolio:
Showcase using Framework 1 presented in this chapter

Audience:
Principal and herself

Developer:
Carolyn Smith, teacher

Assessment:
For each piece of evidence, there was a short description depicting the link between the evidence, domain, and, in appropriate places, student learning outcomes. A reflection was written on the entire experience, outlining strengths and futuristic goals. After the principal reviewed the portfolio, a conference was held between the principal and Carolyn. The purpose of the conference was for the teacher to talk about her portfolio and to clarify any questions or concerns of the principal. The principal gave feedback about each area.

Note: Carolyn Smith presents a very comprehensive portfolio. The amount of evidence may vary for other developers, depending on the subject(s) taught.

Outline of Evidence by Domains Using Framework 1—Relationship to District Evaluation Instrument Categories

1. Discipline, teaching methods, and strategies—focuses on content, units, lessons taught, teaching, learning strategies, and student learning.

Evidence:
   a. Picture of class
   b. Year-long planning guide showing units divided by grading period—this provides the overview for the rest of the evidence

Portfolio Sample 1—continued

because of its organization and detail. Following it are documents that support the year-long planning guide. This class is literature based (evidence c.–h.)

  c. Morning work—student samples

  d. Pictures of modeled writing lessons with student work that includes all steps in the writing cycle

  e. Pictures of buddy readers (daily activity)

FIGURE 6–7 Smith Evidence 1e: Students buddy read as one strategy in my classroom.

  f. Pictures and student work samples from different stories read throughout the year

  g. Pictures showing how the teacher's assistant is used in class

  h. Pictures of a guest speaker as a follow-up to reading a story

  i. Science fair pictures

  j. Field trip brochure

  k. Graphs showing results of class science experiments

  l. Science labs

  m. Pictures of various strategies used in class

Portfolio Sample 1—continued

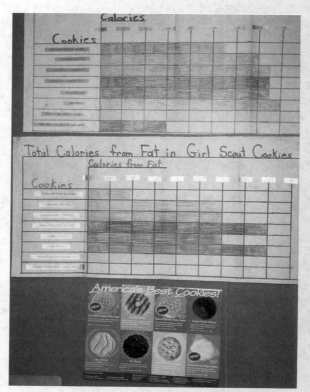

FIGURE 6–8   Smith Evidence 1k: Students do "cookie exploration experiment" in science.

n. Pictures of peer tutors at work
o. Copy of verification log showing students reading 30 minutes a day
2. Class Environment—focuses on organization and structure of the classroom.
   a. Pictures of bulletin boards
   b. Daily learning calendar for science (photocopy)
   c. Pictures of classroom
   d. Behavior and homework charts
   e. Motivation homework pass for one "free" night with no homework
   f. Daily communication letter to parents (for problems)
   g. "Stick" self-discipline program (each day students receive four sticks, taken away if they misbehave; all students who keep sticks all day get a small prize).
   h. Birthday celebration pictures
   i. Supplementary reading incentives program
   j. Student-of-the-week certificate and bulletin board

Portfolio Sample 1—continued

      k. Description of class service project
      l. Parent communication examples (letters, conference sign-up, newsletters)

3. Preparation and Organization—focuses on planning instruction.
      a. Grade-level meeting documentation
      b. Student information sheet
      c. Copies of lesson plan book for 1 week
      d. Copies of a 1-month planning guide (planning meetings by grade level)
      e. Unit guide

4. Student Evaluation—focuses on student assessment.
      a. Checklist for writing assignments
      b. Weekly reports sent to parents
      c. Graphic organizers used by students
      d. Examples of traditional tests
      e. Worksheet
      f. Differentiated test for special needs learner
      g. Sample of grade book
      h. Accelerated Reader report
      i. Science lab write-ups

5. Other School Involvement—focuses on other responsibilities carried out by a teacher.
      a. Home School Relations Committee pictures
      b. Pictures of teacher working with other beginning teachers

FIGURE 6–9   Smith Evidence 5b: Carolyn Smith works with her university intern.

Portfolio Sample 1—continued

   c. School service learning project organization
   d. Cards and letters expressing thanks for different levels of involvement (attending PTA, helping someone, etc.)
   e. Letter from principal thanking Carolyn for committee involvement
   f. Professional organization membership card

Portfolio Sample 2

Nicole Byrd-Phelps is a K–12 music teacher in a small, rural district. Each week she teaches general music to all elementary students and band and chorus at a small high school. This is her 7th year of teaching in the same school where she is tenured. This is her 1st year developing a portfolio.

Purpose:
To demonstrate knowledge, abilities, and disposition as a professional.

Type of Portfolio:
Product using Framework 2, presented earlier in this chapter. Each teacher was required to place certain evidence in each domain. Sample evidence could also be added.

Developer:
Nicole Byrd-Phelps

Audience:
Principal and teacher

Organization:
By domains using Framework 2 (two categories)

Category 1:
Teaching, Learning, and Assessing Content Knowledge

Required Evidence:
   a. Goal and objectives chosen from the state curriculum
   b. A unit of study using various teaching and learning strategies
   c. A videotape of one or more teaching episodes
   d. Sample student work
   e. Reflection

Nicole's required evidence:
   a. Unit focus: Sound for Elementary School Students
   b. Videotape of class activities during the sound unit
   c. Detailed lesson plans from the unit

Portfolio Sample 2—continued

    d. Sample work on videotape (sound activities)
    e. Formal test taken by students
    f. Reflection on Domain 1

Optional Evidence for Domain 1:
    a. Newspaper articles about band and chorus presentations
    b. Band and chorus concert programs (many)
    c. Certificates from band and chorus competitions
    d. Log of after-school music activities

Category 2: Classroom Climate
Required Evidence:
    a. Classroom rules and consequences
    b. List of motivating strategies used in the classroom
    c. Documentation of parent contact
    d. Discipline log
    e. Reflection

Nicole's required evidence:
    a. Band, chorus, and general music rules and consequences
    b. Rewards and incentives (tangible and nontangible) for motivating
       students
    c. Grading system
    d. Parent–student agreement letter
    e. Band and chorus handbooks
    f. Chorus schedule
    g. Sample parent letters
    h. Discipline record with consequences
    i. Parent contact log

Nicole's Domain 1 Reflection
Domain 1 encompasses teaching, learning, and assessing content knowledge. As teachers, we are responsible for knowing our subject matter and being able to present it in an interesting, motivating fashion. Evidence of mastery of one's subject area includes prepared units of study that encompass a variety of teaching strategies, a videotape of one teaching in a highly motivating manner, and examples of student work.

    In my school district, teachers' continuous growth and enhancement in knowledge of their subject areas through professional development activities is a goal. Furthermore, in our school's mission statement, there is a reference to students being able to experience "the joy of learning" at our school. Therefore, to fulfill this goal, it is important for me, as a teacher, to constantly add to my extensive knowledge and to keep learning how to present it better.

Portfolio Sample 2—continued

>   In order to show mastery of the subject matter, I have included pictures, programs, and newspaper articles, which relate events in which my students or I have participated. Some of the pictures and articles show my students participating in events that reflect their acquisition of musical knowledge and performance skills. My abilities and achievements are shown in instances where I am pictured, discussed, or acknowledged. Though I did not have to include these items, I thought they would illustrate what has been happening in my teaching career since its beginning 7 years ago. It is humbling to see the good things that have been accomplished, and I am very thankful for the progress of the music program at the high school and my progress as a teacher.
>
>   I have included a list of after-school activities that I have coordinated as the music director at both schools. The list comprises after-school practices, performances, PTA meetings at which students have performed, and individual help sessions. I have also included a unit of study on sound, which is used in general music classes. I feel that it reflects good integration of science and music.
>
>   I feel that my mastery of musical subject matter is superior. My evaluations offer proof of this. I enjoy learning more about music, and this continued thirst for knowledge will result in my continuous acquisition of knowledge and sharing it with my students. The level of my students does not allow me to teach everything I would like. I must perform a variety of activities for them to understand one concept, so there is not a lot of time for extra things, such as music history or theory. Due to our extensive number of performances, we spend a lot of time at the high school level learning and practicing different songs. "Products" win out over the "process method" of learning music due to time constraints and limited enrollment, reflected in the size of the school (less than 150 students in Grades 6 through 12).
>
>   As I continue to teach, I hope to improve my teaching processes so that students can sight read better and thus learn music more quickly. I also intend to add some software programs and other teaching aids to my general music class. These should spur interest and make learning fun. Hopefully, by continuing to upgrade my instructional methods, I will have extremely musically literate students who are excited about communicating the value of their musical experiences to others.

Portfolio Sample 3: Professional Goal

Rebecca is an elementary school teacher who set increased use of technology as a professional goal.

Purpose:
To demonstrate that a professional goal is met

Type of Portfolio:
Product using Professional Goal Framework

Portfolio Sample 3: Professional Goal—continued

Organization:
By goal(s)

Developer:
Teacher

Audience:
Principal and teacher

Professional Goal—Sample 1 (Rebecca):
To increase technological competency and apply it in the classroom

Evidence:
1. Certificates of technology workshops attended
2. Sample technology products
3. Lesson plans that incorporate technology
4. Student technology products

Portfolio Sample 4: Professional Goal

Tom is a high school health teacher whose district is implementing quality education initiatives. His professional goal reflects a district goal of implementing quality tools in each classroom.

Professional Goal—Sample 2 (Tom):
To incorporate quality tools (plus/delta charts, fishbone problem-solving designs) into the classroom

Evidence:
1. Lesson plans showing quality tools as part of the lesson
2. Student work using quality tools
3. Sample plus/delta charts and fish diagrams from whole class discussions
4. Changes incorporated in the classroom or lessons based on whole class discussions

CLOSING THOUGHTS

Teachers who create portfolios as an alternative evaluation method learn many things about themselves. Over the past 4 years, hundreds of teachers have been assisted by the authors in developing portfolios. Common responses are: "I like being in charge of myself"; "I learned more about my teaching than all of the years I was observed put together"; and "I could clearly see my own strengths and weaknesses based on evidence and the reflection process." Finally, "Creating a portfolio made me look forward to year 30—I wish I had kept a portfolio since year 1, imagine my growth."(Carolyn Smith, a teacher for 31 years, 1998).

The process of creating a portfolio in the 5th, 10th, 20th, or 30th year of teaching can rejuvenate teachers and give them autonomy to help them grow professionally—something that is invaluable as a teacher.

WEB SITES

Faculty Portfolio Development
http://www.utep.edu/cetal/portfoli/

Guide to Connecticut's Best Program for Beginning Teachers
www.csde.state.ct.us

Preparing a Teaching Portfolio—A Guidebook for Texas
http://www.utexas.edu/academic/cte/teachfolio.html

REFERENCES

Danielson, C. (2002). *Enhancing student achievement: A framework for school improvement.* Alexandria, VA: Association for Supervision and Curriculum Development.

Dietz, M. (1995). Using portfolios for a framework for professional development. *Journal of Staff Development, 16*(2), 40–43.

Glatthorn, A. A. (1998a). *Performance assessment and standards-based curricula: The assessment cycle.* Thousand Oaks, CA: Corwin Press.

Glatthorn, A. (1998b). *The teacher's portfolio: Fostering and documenting professional development.* Rockport, MA: ProActive Publications.

Hunter, A. (1998). The power, production, and promise of portfolios for novice and seasoned teachers. In M. McLaughlin, M. E. Vogt, J. Anderson, J. DuMez, M. Peter, & A. Hunter, *Professional portfolio models: Applications in education.* Norwood, MA: Christopher-Gordon.

Jaeger, R. M., & Wrightman, L. F. (1999). Analysis of the reliability of and degree of adverse impact resulting from use of the 1997–1998 pilot test version of the North Carolina Performance-Based Teacher Licensure System: Preliminary report (North Carolina Contract No. 0800008119). Raleigh, NC: Department of Public Instruction.

Jaeger, R. M., & Wrightman, L. F. (2000). *Performance-based licensure handbook.* Raleigh, NC: Department of Public Instruction.

Jaeger, R. M., & Wrightman, L. F. (1996). Performance Assessment Instrument. New York: Teach for America.

Langer, G. (1995). Teacher portfolio assessment. *Education Update, 37*(3), 3.

Linn, R. L., & Gronlund, N. E. (1995). *Measurement and assessment in teaching* (7th ed., pp. 249–257). Upper Saddle River, NJ: Merrill.

Sparks, D. (1997). An interview with Linda Darling-Hammond. *Journal of Staff Development, 18*(1), 34–36.

Wolf, K. (1991). The schoolteacher's portfolio: Issues in design, implementation, and evaluation. *Phi Delta Kappan, 3,* 129–136.

Wolf, K., Lichtenstein, G., & Stevenson, C. (1997). Portfolios in teacher evaluation. In J. Stronge (Ed.), Evaluating teaching: A guide to current thinking and best practice. Thousand Oaks, CA: Corwin Press.

CHAPTER 7

Portfolios for Master Teachers

The capstone event for teachers developing a portfolio is the National Board certification experience. Teachers who are nationally board certified are considered master teachers. The National Board for Professional Teaching Standards (NBPTS) is an independent, nonprofit, nonpartisan organization. In 1986, the Carnegie Corporation's Task Force on Teaching as a Profession released the report *A Nation Prepared: Teachers for the 21st Century*. This report recommended the establishment of the NBPTS. Based on this action and recommendations in *A Nation Prepared* (a follow-up to *A Nation at Risk*), the NBPTS was established in 1987. This organization is governed by a 63-member board of directors, the majority of whom are classroom teachers. The mission of the NBPTS is to establish high and rigorous standards for what accomplished teachers should know and be able to do and then certify those teachers who meet these standards. The thrust of this mission is to improve student learning in American schools by improving teaching through continued reform (NBPTS, 1998).

The NBPTS makes a difference in how district, university, and state department personnel perceive teachers and, most important, how teachers view themselves. The National Board certified (NBC) teacher must be a reflective practitioner who can identify his or her strengths and weaknesses and show the impact of teaching practices on students' learning (http://www.nbpts.org). Barbara B. Kelley, a physical education teacher in Bangor, Maine, and chair of the NBPTS, states, "These candidates serve as excellent role models for their students by being lifelong learners" (Rose, 1999, p. 4). Many unions were hesitant to support the NBC process when it began but have changed their minds. Negotiations for support groups and fee reimbursements for applications are prevalent in unions across the country. Teacher's unions are beginning to see the NBC process as another mechanism to raise teacher professionalism and salaries (Rose, 1999). Even if unions do not support or discourage the NBC process, teachers should review NBPTS materials and decide for themselves because the process is voluntary. All information found by the authors indicated positive effects for teachers who went through the process.

THE FOUNDATION BELIEFS OF THE NBPTS

The National Board for Professional Teaching Standards is based on five propositions of accomplished teaching.* NBC teachers enhance student learning and demonstrate the high level of knowledge, skills, abilities, and commitments reflected in the five core propositions.

Proposition 1:   **Teachers are committed to students and their learning.**

Major Tenets

Accomplished teachers:

1. Are dedicated to making knowledge accessible to all students
2. Believe all students can learn
3. Treat students equitably, recognizing individual differences and reflecting students' diverse needs in practice
4. Understand how students develop and learn
5. Incorporate cognitive and intelligence theories into practice
6. Are aware of contextual and cultural influences
7. Develop students' cognitive capacity and their respect for learning
8. Foster students' self-esteem, motivation, character, and civic responsibility, and their respect for individual, cultural, religious, and racial differences

Proposition 2: **Teachers know the subjects they teach and how to teach them to students.**

Major Tenets

Accomplished teachers:

1. Have a rich understanding of the subject(s) they teach and appreciate how knowledge in their subject is created, linked to other disciplines, and applied to real-world settings
2. Develop the critical and analytical capacities of their students
3. Command specialized knowledge of how to convey and reveal subject matter to students
4. Are aware of the preconceptions and background knowledge that students bring to each subject
5. Are aware of strategies and instructional materials that are appropriate

6. Modify practice according to students' difficulties
7. Create multiple paths to knowledge
8. Teach students how to pose and solve their own problems

Proposition 3: **Teachers are responsible for managing and monitoring student learning.**

Major Tenets

Accomplished teachers:

1. Create, enrich, maintain, and alter instructional settings to capture and sustain the interest of their students and to make the most effective use of time
2. Are adept at engaging students and colleagues to assist in their teaching
3. Command a range of generic instructional techniques and know when to use each one
4. Are aware of ineffectual or damaging practice
5. Know how to engage students
6. Know how to organize instruction so schools' goals are met
7. Are adept at setting norms for social interaction among students and between students and teachers
8. Understand how to motivate students and maintain their interest
9. Can assess the progress of individual students and the whole class
10. Can employ multiple methods for measuring student growth
11. Can clearly explain student performance to parents

Proposition 4: **Teachers think systematically about their practice and learn from experience.**

Major Tenets

Accomplished teachers:

1. Are models of educated persons, exemplifying the virtues they seek to inspire in students—curiosity, tolerance, honesty, fairness, respect for diversity, and appreciation of cultural differences
2. Have the ability to reason and take multiple perspectives to be creative and take risks
3. Can adopt an experimental and problem-solving orientation
4. Draw on their knowledge of human development, subject matter, and instruction, and their understanding of students to make principled judgments about their practice
5. Make decisions based on literature and experience
6. Engage in lifelong learning
7. Strive to strengthen their teaching
8. Critically examine their practice
9. Seek to expand their repertoire, deepen their knowledge, sharpen their judgment, and adapt their teaching to new findings, ideas, and theories

Proposition 5: Teachers are members of learning communities.

Major Tenets

Accomplished teachers:

1. Contribute to the effectiveness of the school by working collaboratively with other professionals on instructional policy, curriculum development, and staff development
2. Can evaluate school progress and the allocation of school resources in relation to state and local educational objectives
3. Are knowledgeable about specialized school and community resources for students' benefit and can employ resources as needed
4. Work collaboratively and creatively with parents, engaging them productively in the work of the school (NBPTS, 1998)

THE STANDARDS

Standards based on the five propositions are developed in over 30 areas. Teachers wishing to seek National Board certification should review all related standards to see which set best correlates with their teaching assignment. There are individual standards for each area of certification. While many sets of NBC standards have similarities, because components of teaching are similar across content and age spans, each individual set of standards is specific for the area of certification. Therefore, careful review of standards is important.

One Set of Standards: Early Childhood–Generalist

I. **Understanding Young Children:** Accomplished early childhood teachers use their knowledge of child development and their relationships with children and families to understand children as individuals and plan their response to unique needs and potentials.

II. **Equity, Fairness, and Diversity:** Accomplished early childhood teachers model and teach behaviors appropriate in a diverse society by creating a safe, secure learning environment for all children; by showing appreciation of and respect for the individual differences and unique needs of each member of the learning community; and by empowering children to treat others with, and to expect from others, equity, fairness, and dignity.

III. **Assessment:** Accomplished early childhood teachers recognize the strengths and weaknesses of multiple assessment methodologies and know how to use them effectively. Employing a variety of methods, they systematically observe, monitor, and document children's activities and behavior, analyzing, communicating, and using the information they glean to improve their work with children, parents, and others.

IV. **Promoting Child Development and Learning:** Accomplished early childhood teachers promote children's cognitive, social, emotional, physical, and linguistic development by organizing and orchestrating the environment in ways that best facilitate the development and learning of young children.

V. **Knowledge of Integrated Curriculum:** Based on their knowledge of how young children learn, of academic subjects, and of assessment, accomplished early childhood teachers design and implement developmentally appropriate learning experiences that integrate within and across the disciplines.

VI. **Multiple Teaching Strategies for Meaningful Learning:** Accomplished early childhood teachers use a variety of practices and resources to promote individual development, meaning learning, and social cooperation.

VII. **Family and Community Partnerships:** Accomplished early childhood teachers work with and through families and communities to support children's learning and development.

VIII. **Professional Partnerships:** Accomplished early childhood teachers work as leaders and collaborators in the professional community to improve programs and practices for young children and their families.

IX. **Reflective Practice:** Accomplished early childhood teachers regularly analyze, evaluate, and synthesize to strengthen the quality and effectiveness of their work. (NBPTS, 2003)

Similar standards are developed for specific categories. The purpose of the standards is to make the propositions specific to the discipline. When creating the National Board portfolio, a teacher should keep the standards and propositions foremost in his or her mind.

WHO CAN APPLY?

Candidates must hold a bachelor's degree, have completed 3 years of classroom teaching, and hold a valid teaching license. One must also teach at the pre-K–12 level, not in a community college or university.

TIME LINE

Teachers apply for their National Board packet and complete the requirements over a 6 to 9 month period at their school site. Individuals have a minimum of 5 months to complete activities. Candidates can apply in one of three cycles. They can register between April 1 and June 30 and have a portfolio deadline of February 15. Those who apply from July 1 through September 30 will complete their work by March 15, and those who apply from October 1 to December 31 will meet an April 15 due date. Interested parties should check specific certification areas for more detail and should also check with the National Board about their specific area of interest. Candidates must turn in initial verification documentation within a few weeks of receiving the packet. Look for this information immediately and return the correct forms. Teachers report they spend about 120 hours compiling their portfolios. Notification of certification status comes approximately 6 months after all parts have been completed. National Board certification is valid for 10 years (NBPTS, 1998).

What Is Required?

While each certification area requires different activities that specifically correlate to the standards, each asks for the same general requirements:

1. Two or three classroom-based activities with student work samples
2. A videotape that correlates with one or more of the classroom-based activities
3. Work outside the classroom with parents, families, colleagues, and communities
4. Documented accomplishments as a professional
5. Written reflections on each activity

The National Board assesses a teacher's performance based on three types of evidence, which is submitted in the form of separate entries. The three types of evidence are:

- Samples of students' work
- Videotapes of classroom practice
- Documentation of accomplishments outside the classroom (NBPTS, 2003)

Early Childhood–Generalist Activities
Entry 1—Examining Children's Literacy Development

Two children are selected, and sample work is collected to show the teacher's work with children in fostering literacy development. The assessment of children's abilities and needs, response to that assessment in the design and implementation of instruction, and selected work samples demonstrating the children's literacy development are the focus of this entry.

Entry 2—Building a Classroom Community

A videotape and instructional materials that demonstrate the knowledge and ability to deepen students' understanding of a social studies topic, concept, or theme are submitted. Also required are the ability to integrate the arts and demonstration of the teacher's interaction with children during group discussion or activities that illustrate the ability to create a classroom climate that promotes children's development of social and interpersonal skills.

Entry 3—Integrating Mathematics and Science

Instructional materials and a videotape of an integrative learning experience designed to deepen children's understanding of mathematical and scientific concepts through a "big idea" in science are required for submission. Candidates must show the development of skills in using mathematical and scientific ways of observing, thinking, and communicating.

Entry 4—Documented Accomplishments: Contributions to Student Learning

The illustration of partnerships with students' families and community and the candidate's development as a learner and collaborator with other professionals are required. These are evidenced through descriptions and documentation of activities and accomplishments in these areas (NBPTS, 2003).

What Are Other Things to Know About Evidence?

Several of the activities for each set of standards require supporting evidence, deemed *artifacts* in the NBPTS literature. There are several things to keep in mind when compiling evidence:

1. The artifacts you feature in different entries must come from different units of instruction, different lessons, and different points in time. In other words, what you use with one entry needs to be different from what you use for another entry.
2. No artifact may be larger than 8.5 inches by 11 inches.
3. Do not send any three-dimensional artifacts or original artwork—photograph them.
4. One photograph is equivalent to one artifact.
5. Do not submit videotapes (beyond the required one) or audiotapes—transcribe relevant conversations.
6. Do not send class sets of work; a work sample from one child counts as one artifact.
7. Delete the last names of children or any identifying information about their families.
8. Label each artifact with a number placed in the upper righthand corner. Use this number in the Written Commentary when referring to the artifact.
9. Date the artifact. In the Written Commentary, include the date the artifact was created and an explanation of its significance to the points you have made, for example: Artifact 2 is an anecdotal record on my observations of children constructing the city. I noted that they did not understand that the water supply needed to be elevated because of the lack of sufficient natural waterpower. As a result, I elaborated on the concept the following day. (NBPTS, 2003)

NATIONAL BOARD ASSESSMENT CENTER EXERCISES

The second part of National Board certification is the assessment center exercises. This written test is based on challenging teacher issues and includes evaluating other practices, interviews, and content exams in a teacher's field. Each year, there is a "window," usually during the summer, when this written assessment must be taken. This window is usually between 2 and 4 weeks, depending on the area of certification. Each of the certification areas have the following assessment center characteristics in common:

1. There are six exercises.
2. Candidates have 30 minutes to respond to each exercise.
3. In most areas, exercises are delivered on a computer screen. In the areas of Music and World Languages Other Than English, all exercises are not delivered on the computer due to the nature of the content.
4. Exercises are across the entire certification area.

Good Information About the Written Assessment

1. This assessment is taken at Sylvan Assessment Centers and Thomson Prometric Testing Centers (1-800-967-1100) across the country.
2. Candidates must reserve a day for their assessment in advance.
3. The center exercises are usually six 30-minute essays, which test knowledge and practical application of standards.
4. Candidates can take the written assessment using paper and pencil or on a computer. One should think about the type of test he or she is taking. If it will contain math symbols, paper and pencil might be easier unless one is extremely computer literate.
5. The tests are timed.
6. Candidates may answer using connected paragraphs or through bulleted lists. The important consideration is that candidates convey their answers clearly.
7. Candidates need to clearly answer questions for each exercise.
8. Specific detail and clarity help assessors see direct correlations between answers and the standards that are addressed.

Assessment Center Exercise Description for Young Adolescent Mathematics

Background:
The Adolescence and Young Adulthood/Mathematics certificate is designed for teachers of high school students. Teachers who receive this certification have displayed their competency in ways that reflect on their practice, create a climate that supports learning, develop curriculum, analyze student work, assess and support the growth of students, and form partnerships with parents and colleagues. Candidates complete two components, a portfolio with four entries and an assessment center evaluation with six exercises. Goals for several of the assessment center exercises are briefly described below. This could be in the form of developing curriculum, giving examples, or other related work. Candidates would have 30 minutes for each exercise.

Exercise 1: Algebra
Candidates will demonstrate knowledge of the foundation of algebra using several of the mathematical thinking processes in reasoning about concepts such as functional relations, modeling situations, and representing numerical patterns and quantitative relationships in various forms. They will also show understanding of content knowledge through identification of fundamental instructional concerns in this area.

Exercise 2: Calculus
Using several of the mathematical thinking processes in reasoning about calculus, candidates will show how to work with limits, derivatives, integrals, and infinite series, and apply these concepts to other mathematical concepts, such as measuring and analyzing rates of change, optimization, and the accumulation of continuously varying quantities. They will also show understanding of content knowledge through the identification of fundamental instructional concerns in this area.

Exercise 3: Discrete Mathematics
Using several of the mathematical thinking processes, candidates will exhibit reasoning about concepts such as finite differences, algorithms, sequences and formal series, recursion, iteration, proof by induction, matrices, graphs and networks, counting techniques, finite probability, elements of number theory, and modular systems.

Exercise 4: Geometry
Using several of the mathematical thinking processes, candidates will demonstrate reasoning about shape, size, measure, position, patterns, transformations, and geometric relations. They will also show understanding of content knowledge through identification of fundamental instructional concerns in this area.

Assessment Center Exercise Description for
Young Adolescent Mathematics—continued

Exercise 5: Statistics and Data Analysis
Using several of the mathematical thinking processes, candidates will demonstrate reasoning about data analysis and statistics. Teachers will describe, represent, and interpret statistical data as well as statistical inference. They will also show understanding of content knowledge through identification of fundamental instructional concerns in this area.

Exercise 6: Technology and Manipulatives
Using technology and manipulatives, candidates will show how to support and facilitate the appropriate development of skills and understanding within the core domains of mathematical knowledge (NBPTS, 2003).

From these descriptions, one can see that several things are emphasized in the assessment center exercises. These would include the knowledge of content, the understanding of students' strengths and areas of concern in relation to the content, different areas of mathematics, and the continued use of mathematical thinking processes. Notice how definite areas of the mathematics curriculum are covered in the six exercises previously outlined. The primary focus of the assessment center exercises is the verification of content knowledge.

ASSESSMENT AND EVALUATION

Teachers are trained to assess the portfolio and assessment center exercises. Professional teachers apply to be assessors and are trained extensively to judge portfolios accurately. Scoring is based on all of the candidate's responses—videotapes, student work samples, written documentary, and center exercises. The key to assessment is meeting the standards. Criteria for assessment are based on the standards. When a developer is reviewing his or her portfolio, the standards should be referred to consistently. Each activity and center exercise receives a score. If a section is not passed, the score can be banked. Teachers may redo any portfolio activity or center exercise and submit it to be rescored.

It is important for candidates to make sure each portfolio activity is complete. When packing the portfolio, each activity is put in a separate envelope. These activities are assessed separately. Evaluators will not know a teacher's students, school, or other demographics, so one should be specific (North Carolina Association of Educators [NCAE], 1998).

Scoring Specifics

Assessors use guiding questions and rubrics to assess portfolio activities. Guiding questions reflect the standards. The guiding questions are designed to help assessors focus on the exact nature of the candidate's materials and determine the ways in which they reflect the criteria in the directions and in the rubric.

New NBC areas are scored by two assessors, a process called double scoring. This practice is followed for 1 year. Certification areas that have been offered for at least 1 year are scored using modified double scoring. This means that 25% of the entries are double-scored and 75% are single scored. The National Board commission has found no significant differences in the results using the modified system of scoring. In the double-scoring system, if two scores for a response differ by more than 1.25, then the performance is scored a third time by the trainer of the assessors. In cases where two scores are assigned, they are averaged. If the trainer has to evaluate a candidate's performance, a third reading, the weighted average, is computed by doubling the trainer's score, adding the two assessors' scores, and dividing by 4. The degree of assessor reliability reported by NBPTS assessments is considered by measurement experts to be among the highest for such a complex system (NBPTS, 2003).

Throughout the scoring process, assessors use specific documents to evaluate candidate responses. These include:

1. The *standards*, the foundation document for the assessment process
2. The *instructions* for the entry and exercise, especially the questions given to the candidates to shape their written commentaries for the portfolio entry
3. A *note-taking guide* that provides each assessor with a framework of specific entry questions to use in recording and evaluating evidence in the process of scoring
4. The *rubric* for each entry and exercise that has specific terminology
5. The *benchmarks* for each entry and exercise, which are actual performances at each point on the scoring scale that clearly demonstrate the characteristics
6. The *exercise scoring record* for each entry and exercise, which provides a space for assessors to record and organize evidence

There is a 4-point holistic rubric for each activity that contains terminology that reflects performance. The wording is precise. Four words help define criteria in the rubrics:

Convincing speaks to the specificity of the evidence, connections made to its importance by the teacher, the appropriateness of the reasons for actions, and the inferences the teacher gives.

Consistent speaks to how the evidence from all sources conveys a coherent picture of the teacher's practice.

Convincing and significant speaks to whether the evidence is important. Does evidence from all sources support the judgment that this is an accomplished practitioner? Is the description precise, specific, and detailed?

Plausible   speaks to the believability of the evidence, given the assessor's professional expertise and experience. This is in relation to standards and reasonable expectations. (NCAE, 1998)

Sample Portfolio Language Framework

Standards for each entry are reflected throughout the portfolio as well:

Level 4: clear, consistent, convincing, accurate reflection of what is there
Level 3: clear evidence, but not as strongly or clearly articulated, less detailed
Level 2: limited evidence, vague goals
Level 1: little or no evidence or goals; items missing or weak; little or no reflection about students; rationale missing, weak, or unrelated (NCAE, 1998)

Specific Evaluation Criteria

Specific criteria are reflected throughout all activity rubrics. It includes:

- Knowledge of students: specific, detailed, individualized
- High expectations for student achievement in the context of the particular class
- Appropriate goals or activities for a particular class and students
- Worthwhile goals or activities for a particular class and goals for the activities
- Insightful or perceptive analysis

Scoring

The scale score has four ordinal points, ranging from low (1) to high (4). In addition, assessors use pluses and minuses to indicate gradations of performance that cannot be represented by the scale scores (e.g., .75, 1.0, 1.25, 1.75, 2.0, 2.25, etc.; NBPTS, 1998).

OTHER RELEVANT INFORMATION

1. Applications are available by calling or writing the NBPTS at 1-800-22-TEACH; www.nbpts.org; National Board for Professional Teaching Standards, 26555 Evergreen Road, Suite 400, Southfield, MI 48076.

2. The application fee is $2,300. A minimum of $500 is due with the application.

3. Sample portfolios are available for purchase from the NBPTS. Before one pays $2,300, it might be helpful to order one of these.

4. Different states have various incentives and financial support for National Board certification. For example, North Carolina pays for the fee and gives teachers a 12% raise. Mississippi NBC teachers who are employed receive a $3,000 salary supplement and the certification fee is reimbursed. Many other states offer scholarships or partial reimbursements for application fees

through grants and other monies. School districts within various states also give incentives often above those offered by state legislatures.

5. Thirty states pay the fee in full for teachers, while several others cover half the fee. Teachers can also receive low-interest loans from NEA member benefits.

6. Thirty-three percent to 40% of candidates are successful on their first try (NCAE, 1998).

7. Over 36 states recognize National Board certification for licensure.

8. Thirty-five states and the District of Columbia waive part of their licensing requirements for National Board certified teachers (Loschert, 2003).

TIPS AND GOOD INFORMATION FROM NATIONALLY CERTIFIED TEACHERS

There are many things that can help a teacher be successful in this process:

1. A teacher should apply for the appropriate area. Reviewing standards for various areas will help a candidate determine the category in which to apply for best results.

2. General descriptions of activities for each set of standards can help make the decision. If a candidate can't think of an activity that would be appropriate for each activity, then he or she should look at a different set of standards. Many overlap, so a candidate should not "make up" or "force" any lessons or student work for any activity.

3. Create a support network. Tell students and administrators. Ask family members for support. Don't take on extra responsibilities during this time.

4. Go to one of many workshops offered to determine if this is the process for you.

5. Enlist a colleague to work toward National Board certification with you. He or she will provide the best incentive for you to finish.

6. Plan some milestones and celebrations during the 5 months.

7. Make a plan and stick with it. First, review units and choose those that best fit the activities. Schedule time to work on your activities each week.

8. Plant a video camera in the classroom. Let the students get used to it.

9. Find a proofreader who will be honest. Make sure this person will invest the time needed (6–8 hours) and give constructive feedback.

10. Once the box of materials is received, read everything.

11. Keep the box. Activities are packed in it to return for scoring.

12. Fill out the initial paperwork when it arrives. It is due soon.

13. Use a highlighter to outline important instructions.

14. Carry a pad around to jot down ideas and record reflections. Put it by your bed, because many times the best ideas come in the middle of the night.

15. Put a box in the classroom to put samples and other evidence in that might be helpful later.

16. Buy Post-it notes to use on planning charts (supplied in the portfolio box). If a candidate changes his or her mind, then the planning idea can be changed.

17. Keep portfolios of student work samples—not just the best work but a variety of student work.

18. Keep a loaded camera in the classroom. A disposable one will work if it has a flash.

19. Keep a journal. Practice writing reflections before doing portfolio reflections.

20. Keep a phone log of parent communications.

21. Voices must be heard on the videotape. Do a sample run.

22. Label the videotape with the date and a related entry.

23. Inform the school office and put a sign on your door when you are videotaping. Remember, the video camera cannot be stopped, so interruptions can hinder a candidate.

24. Get on the contact list for support. Applicants are sent a list of all candidates for that year. Call your colleagues.

25. Read everything and organize it into a three-ring notebook.

26. Get student release forms signed and returned immediately. Candy works well as an incentive.

27. Each candidate receives a number. Print pages of these on "crack and peel" adhesive paper to stick on each page.

28. Set aside an entire day to fill out the form and package the product.

29. Use a lot of self-talk. This is time-consuming but worthwhile.

30. Break down entries. Tackle one at a time.

31. Begin early and stick with it.

REFLECTIONS

In the National Board process, the reflection is called a written commentary. Usually, these commentaries are approximately 10 pages. The written commentary contains three types of writing: description, analysis, and reflection. Descriptions should be clear and precise, especially with entries that have no accompanying videotapes. A candidate must paint a picture for the assessor. The analysis section answers the question, Why? Why are lessons taught in a certain way? How and in what way are things carried out in the classroom? Reflection is the self-analysis section. What did a candidate infer about his or her practice? What does this entry show about a candidate's teaching? In retrospect, what does the entry show?

Write clearly and to the point. Candidates should add any comments that will help prove that what is shown in the evidence meets the standards. Content is important and should include parallel evidence. A good portfolio will have strong evidence and a convincing commentary; both must relate to the standards (NCAE, 1998).

Other things to know about the written commentary:

1. Word process everything; this way changes will be easier.
2. Stick to the page length; anything over the limit will not be read.
3. Have 1-inch margins on all sides.
4. Double-space the text.
5. Number the pages.
6. Use 10- or 12-point font; font less than 10 points is not allowed.
7. One could use subtitles to break down commentary, but these will be included in the page count. (NBPTS, 1998)

The written commentary is an important component of the portfolio because it provides documentation and clarification for the evidence. Clear, consistent language will help the assessor understand the intent of the candidate.

Sample Directions for Commentary High School Mathematics Entry

Setting the Stage—Background and Standard Information Given in an Entry
Entry 1: Analysis of Student Work: Applications

Accomplished mathematics teachers understand their students and center their classrooms around them. They design lessons considering differing aptitudes, knowledge, interests, and ways of learning. They create situations that encourage students to explore and build on previous knowledge and understanding, and they enable students to recognize the connections among concrete, symbolic, and graphic representations. They create learning experiences in which students analyze a wide range of patterns from all aspects of scientific, technical, and practical work. They use calculators and computers as instructional resources to help students represent and reason about mathematical patterns. They have a broad and deep knowledge of the discipline, of the important mathematical domains, and of the processes of mathematical thinking. They design lessons to engage students in problem solving, mathematical communication, reasoning, and searching for connections. They have a clear understanding of the connections between mathematics and other fields of human endeavor, and connections within the strands of mathematics.

They design their lessons with important mathematical goals and select instructional techniques and activities that allow students to meet them. They make effective judgments related to content choice, sequence, emphasis, and instruction that will facilitate student understanding, communication, and reasoning. They identify, assess, adapt, and create instructional resources to enhance student learning.

They design appropriate and varied strategies to assess processes and products of students' mathematical explorations and problem-solving activities, modify lessons based on assessment results, and provide timely and instructive feedback to students. They reflect on what they teach and how they teach, seeking to improve their knowledge and practice.

Specific Directions

For the entry, teachers must:

- Select three students who represent different kinds of challenges.
- Submit an assignment or prompt that requires students to explore or engages them in making important connections among ideas in mathematics, or between mathematics and contexts outside mathematics to help them better understand the content being studied.
- Submit the responses of the three students selected for this assignment.
- Submit a written commentary of no more than 11 pages that contextualizes, explains, and analyzes this teaching.

The written commentary must address:

- **Instructional Context:** The relevant features of your teaching setting—how the instructional context affects practice. (Suggested length—one page)
- **Planning:** What are the learning objectives? Where does this assignment fit in the instructional sequence for the unit? What is the rationale for using this particular assignment in light of overall learning goals for the lesson, unit, and year? How was the assignment designed to elicit mathematical reasoning and thinking from students? (Suggested length—two pages)
- **Analysis of Three Student Responses:** Why was each student chosen? What challenges do the students represent? What does one need to know about each student to understand the attached response? How does each student's work reflect (or not reflect) the learning objectives? How was feedback given to the students? (Suggested length—six pages)
- **Reflection:** What does each student's work suggest about the teacher's "next steps" in instruction? What would the teacher do differently the next time this lesson was taught (prior to, during, or after)? What would be repeated? Why? (Suggested length—two pages)

CLOSING THOUGHTS

The teacher takes on an exciting goal when he or she decides to apply for National Board certification. Those who want to be successful in this endeavor should understand and embrace the standards in their area. This time-consuming process is valuable to teachers. The process provides a standards-based professional development opportunity for teachers at a point in their careers when evaluation typically becomes routine. It allows teachers to take their experiences and knowledge "to the next level" through self-reflection and evaluation. The impact of reflection will carry over into the next years of teaching. Those who have succeeded have learned much about themselves as teachers and are proud to be called a nationally certified teacher, a title held by a small percentage of the teaching profession.

CHAPTER ACTIVITIES

1. For each of the five NBPTS propositions of accomplished teaching, describe each of the components that you already use in your classroom. If you don't feel that you have properly met one of the propositions, describe ways that you could meet it in the future.
2. Develop activities to meet four or five of the NBC standards.
3. Analyze and reflect on your own teaching abilities and practices. Determine areas that you want to more fully develop when considering the assessment section of the NBC portfolio.
4. What are questions that you could ask yourself while reflecting on the various aspects of the NBC process?

WEB SITE

Official National Board for Professional Teaching Standards Web site
http://www.nbpts.org

REFERENCES

Loschert, K. (2003). Pursuing teaching excellence. *NEA Today, 28*(7), 21.

National Board for Professional Teaching Standards. (1998). *Guide to National Board certification.* Southfield, MI: Author.

National Board for Professional Teaching Standards. (2003). Retrieved from http://www.nbpts.org

North Carolina Association of Educators. (1998). *NBPTS information session and handouts.* Raleigh, NC: Author.

Rose, M. (1999). *American Teacher, 83,* 6–7, 14.

CHAPTER 8

Digital Portfolios

By Dr. Ivan Wallace

One exciting change in portfolio design and development has been the emergence of digital portfolios. There are many advantages to being able to present a digital portfolio depicting every item in an organized fashion and presented digitally without the bulk of a binder, accordion file, or file box. Imagine being able to display any material in your portfolio instantaneously with the click of a button as you benefit from the multimedia capabilities that technology has brought into the classroom. Imagine all of the material in your three-ring binders, file boxes, and accordion files efficiently organized on a space-saving CD-ROM or Web server that affords immediate access from any location. All of these options are surprisingly easy to do using technologies presently available in today's schools. While attempts at developing and keeping digital portfolios are becoming more and more common in K–16 settings, the practice of developing digital portfolios has been in use in many educational environments that have embraced the use of technology at an early stage. An example of this practice is the Department of Education at California State University, which began working on electronic student teaching portfolios in the spring of 1997, with the intended use of documenting growth of the student teacher from the beginning of the teacher preparation program to its end (Guenter, 1998).

DIGITAL PORTFOLIOS

A digital portfolio contains essentially the same material that would be placed in a traditional portfolio. However, these items are captured, organized, saved, and presented in a digital format. The digital portfolio typically contains digital photographs, scanned images, captured screen images, text files, audio files, video files, electronic presentations, and even links to Web resources. Consequently, you have the benefit of the digital portfolio, which may be saved and distributed on a CD-ROM or other large capacity disk, or Web server. Items placed in a digital portfolio may be linked to multiple interactive items that provide reflection, interpretation, or additional detail.

A digital portfolio uses technologies that allow the portfolio developer to collect and organize portfolio artifacts in many digital formats (such as audio, video, graphics, and text). A standards-based portfolio uses a database or hypertext links to clearly show the relationship between the standards or goals, artifacts, and reflections. Often, the terms *electronic portfolio* and *digital portfolio* are used interchangeably; however, there is a distinction: An electronic portfolio contains artifacts that may be in analog form, such as an audio- or videotape, or may be in computer-readable form. In a digital portfolio, all artifacts have been transformed into computer-readable formats.

Digital portfolios may be created in a variety of ways using popular multimedia software packages. They may be commercially available propriety portfolio design software as well as more broad-based multimedia or presentation software packages. Such programs typically provide a template for easily facilitating the development of the portfolio. More daring portfolio designers may use multimedia authoring programs to create their own portfolio template. In addition, digital portfolios may be authored as Web pages using HTML programming or with Web design authoring software, which makes them ideal for instant access by any computer system with a Web browser.

Why Design a Digital Portfolio?

Digital portfolios can offer advantages over traditionally designed versions. These include convenience, interactivity, connectivity, the development of technology skills in the process of assembling the portfolio, and demonstration of those skills to supervisors or potential employers.

In general, portfolios can present a daunting organizational challenge because of the sheer amount of material collected across time and multiplied by the number of performance areas for which material is being collected. While the large volume of evidence may result in material that could complicate its presentation, evaluation, and interpretation if not handled with care, these potential hazards are usually offset by the immediate access, quality of presentation, and professional visual appeal provided by its appearance as digital media.

Digital portfolios represent a medium that can store and organize substantial amounts of material that might otherwise require significant storage space in traditional formats. However, video segments, digital photographs, text, audio files, and scanned materials in digital format may now be easily placed onto a single CD, other high-capacity disk storage media, or an online server. Digital portfolios also can be quickly and inexpensively duplicated so that copies of the originals may be easily disseminated to others.

Organized in a traditional manner (such as three-ring binders or accordion files), portfolios invite linear thinking regarding the collection and presentation of performance evidence and its interpretation. Traditional portfolio devices also often present evidence in domains or by categories. Thus, important connections between pieces of evidence may appear obscure because of relatively rigid categorical systems for storage and presentation. On the contrary, many digital portfolios allow the designer to connect portfolio entries to each other through multiple paths. The result can be an interactive document with entries meaningfully connected. For example, a lesson plan in a digital portfolio could be linked to a PowerPoint presentation that the teacher has designed for delivery to the class or to a short video segment of the activity being conducted during the lesson. Another link on the lesson plan might open multiple windows showing student work produced during the lesson, a photograph of engaged students, or a text, audio, or video reflection. In the digital portfolio, these pieces of evidence are connected to strengthen the viewer's understanding of the lesson.

In addition, the process of designing a digital portfolio offers opportunities to develop and refine important technological skills. There may be special value in mastering technology in the process of constructing a digital portfolio. When experiences with technology are placed in the context of valued activities, the acquisition of these skills occurs more meaningfully. As Watts (1997) has observed, technology becomes a catalyst because "in the struggle to master its use, we have, by necessity, become learners" (p. 30). Building a digital portfolio requires acquiring skill in the use of a variety of types of hardware (scanners, digital cameras, video equipment, storage devices, and computers) as well as image manipulation programs, video editing and compression processes, and multimedia authoring. Technological competencies such as these can continue to increase instructional effectiveness, and creating an electronic portfolio can develop teachers' as well as students' multimedia skills.

There are many reasons to consider using digital portfolios. In summary, the benefits of developing digital portfolios include:

- Accessibility (especially Web portfolios)
- Ease of duplication
- Increased technological skills
- Learner centered

- Long shelf life
- Minimal storage space
- Multiple linkage
- Portability

How Do I Create a Digital Portfolio?

Careful planning is essential in designing and producing a high-quality digital portfolio, just as it is with traditional portfolio design. Good visual skills and a keen understanding of digital file structures are essential for digital portfolio creation. While the quality of any portfolio, whether digital or traditional in format, is determined primarily by the decisions made about content and the reflection on that content, digital portfolios can be adversely affected if evidence is poorly scanned, photos are not cropped properly, audio or video is not done at a professional level of acceptance, or file formats and software used are not universal. In addition, the guidelines and principles governing portfolio content reflection presented in Chapters 4 through 6 apply to digital formats just as they do to building a traditional portfolio. The multimedia development process usually covers the following stages (Ivers & Barron, 1998):

1. *Assess/decide.* The focus is on the needs assessment of the audience, the presentation goals, and the appropriate tools for the final portfolio presentation.
2. *Design/plan.* In the second stage, focus on organizing or designing the presentation. Determine audience-appropriate content, software, storage medium, and presentation sequences. Construct flowcharts and write storyboards.
3. *Develop.* Gather materials to include in the presentation and organize them into a sequence (or use hyperlinks) for the best presentation of the material, using an appropriate multimedia authoring program.
4. *Implement.* The developer presents the portfolio to the intended audience.
5. *Evaluate.* In this final stage of multimedia development, the focus is on evaluating the presentation's effectiveness in light of its purpose and the assessment context.

DIGITAL PORTFOLIO SOFTWARE

Whether the digital portfolio is being designed by a preservice teacher as a university requirement, a teacher as a resume for employment purposes, a beginning teacher as a licensure requirement, or an experienced teacher seeking an alternative to traditional performance evaluation or pursuing National Board certification, similar decisions will guide the design process. There are three basic design options for the digital portfolio. It may be created using (1) propriety digital portfolio software, (2) presentation or multimedia software, or (3) Web-page design software. The option selected for a digital portfolio depends on the content to be placed into it, the uses envisioned for it, and the audiences expected to view it.

Propriety Digital Portfolio Software

A number of programs on the market are designed to provide templates for creating a digital portfolio. Many of these are designed for teachers to create digital portfolios with their students. In addition, these programs may be used to create professional portfolios as well. This software review includes programs designed specifically for professional or preprofessional portfolio design (The Teacher's Portfolio); for the design of portfolios for professionals, preprofessionals, and students (Scholastic Electronic Portfolio); and programs limited to use in developing student portfolios (The Portfolio Assessment Kit and CD-me), a comprehensive, easy-to-use, digital-portfolio creation system with all the information, curriculum, and software templates required to create digital portfolios in any particular environment.

These programs vary considerably with regard to design features. Consider carefully what the digital portfolio should look like and select the program that will produce the desired style. Also, when using proprietary software, it is important to select software from established companies so that your software can be upgraded as newer versions are developed and become available in the future.

• *Scholastic Electronic Portfolio* (Scholastic, Inc., 1995) is one of the more flexible and powerful programs available. It allows the user to create a variety of portfolio designs, including text, time lines, sound, slide shows, video, and launch views. Material from any of these views may be linked to any other material in the portfolio using hot-linked text and buttons. The software is packaged with a detailed manual and a CD containing several model portfolios illustrating the variety of designs possible. Unfortunately, this program is available only for Macintosh. The large number of design options left in the user's control require that some time be spent mastering the program. A tutorial is also provided.

• *The Portfolio Assessment Toolkit* (Forest Technologies) is a multimedia electronic portfolio program that includes three customizable portfolios (primary, intermediate, and secondary) that are adaptable for students and adults of all ages. The software is a companion to HyperStudio. The program contains over 40 ready-made cards to create and customize the portfolio. Goals can be linked to specific projects, scanned materials, and photographs. A built-in sound recorder feature allows audio reflection. The Portfolio Assessment Toolkit is available in both Macintosh and Windows environments.

• *The Portfolio Assessment Kit* (Super School Software) provides a collection of programs that may be used to document student work across time. This multifunctional program is designed primarily to create student portfolios at the elementary level and has limited direct value in the design of professional portfolios.

• *The Portfolio Builder for PowerPoint* (Visions-Technology in Education) is a companion product for PowerPoint users that provides elementary, middle school, secondary, and adult templates for constructing a portfolio. Graphics, sound, video, and text may be combined to create a multimedia portfolio. In addition, the portfolio created with the Portfolio Builder may be published on the Internet. The kit contains student and teacher tutorials, sample products, and the PowerPoint viewer, which allows portfolios to be played on computers without PowerPoint. This program is available for both Windows and Macintosh platforms.

• *The Teacher's Portfolio* (Aurbach & Associates) is a Macintosh software package that can be used by teachers to create and maintain a professional portfolio, by university personnel to perform portfolio-based evaluation for preservice teachers (using INTASC or other standards), and by administrators to perform portfolio-based evaluation of inservice teachers (using INTASC or other standards). The Teacher's Portfolio provides a framework for displaying work in multimedia formats, including sound, graphics, video, text, and computer exhibits. Each portfolio exhibit has specific places for describing the piece, for self-reflection, and for evaluation by the portfolio owner, a supervisor, and a "visitor." A separate Notes section provides room for additional comments or dialog between profile developers and their supervisors or evaluators. The Teacher's Portfolio is shipped with descriptors based on INTASC standards for new teachers, with additional descriptors devised by an advisory board of university professors and school professionals. You may use these descriptors, modify them, or discard them and add your own based on local teaching standards or university requirements. The program has room for 10 separate domains of INTASC standards and two journal cards (one for the portfolio owner and one for the supervisor or evaluator). The Teacher's Portfolio also provides a place for teachers to display their personal information (address, phone, photo, etc.), professional goals, educational philosophy, experience, development activities, competencies, and academic record. The program prints reports, and each portfolio is password protected. Demo versions of the program may be downloaded from *http://www.aurbach.com*.

MULTIMEDIA AND PRESENTATION AUTHORING SOFTWARE

By the sheer nature of their design, multimedia and presentation authoring software lend themselves well for use in digital portfolios, since their entire focus in normal use is on visual design and the use of text, audio, video, and other multimedia objects. While there are many commercial packages on the market, many are rather expensive, which limits their use in an environment where it is intended to be global and to provide unlimited access to those who would consider their applicability to the construction of digital portfolios. Consequently, HyperStudio and PowerPoint are the most widely used software packages in this category, and both have the added advantage of appearing extensively in educational environments over the past several years. They are economically priced, which facilitates their use in unlimited classroom environments. HyperStudio is basically entrenched in the elementary arena, whereas PowerPoint has been used extensively in high schools and universities and is rapidly expanding to the entire K–12 market. Following are summaries of good software programs for portfolios:

- HyperStudio 4.0 is probably the single best choice for authoring one's own portfolio framework. In the past it has been the most widely used multimedia authoring software in the elementary education arena. The user may create connected series of cards with sound, video, text, scanned images, digital photographs, and combinations of the formats. Portfolios created with HyperStudio may be placed online, saved to CD, and viewed across platforms.

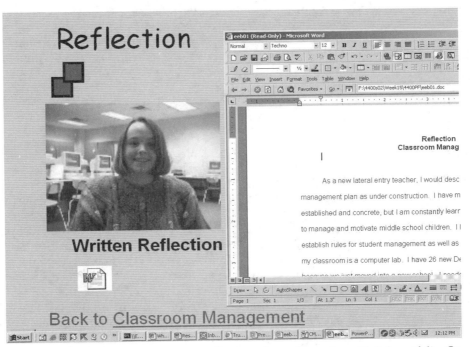

FIGURE 8–1   Example of using PowerPoint as the medium for a digital portfolio. On the reflection page, a Microsoft Word icon serves as the trigger to link to the written reflection that was created as a Word document.

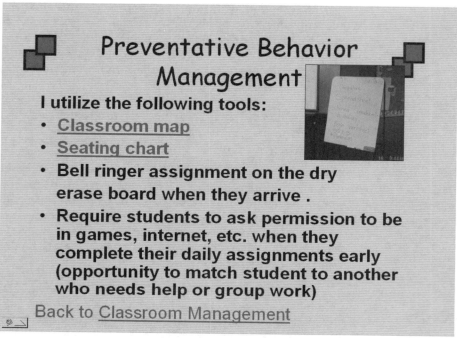

FIGURE 8–2   In this example of a portfolio created in PowerPoint, the underscored words serve as hot links to link to the slides that contain the classroom map and seating chart.

- Astound Presentation 8.0 is a multimedia authoring program designed to support interactive presentations. PowerPoint slides may be imported into Astound portfolios, and these portfolios may be exported to Web pages.
- Microsoft PowerPoint 2002 is probably one of the most popular software packages available in all educational environments today (see Figure 8–1). Consequently, portfolios developed in PowerPoint offer the added advantage of being in a format that is virtually universal and can be accessed by any computer and have a more extended life than portfolios that depend on other priority software for creation and display. PowerPoint provides easy navigation through the use of "Action Settings" that link to other PowerPoint slides or external documents and files. Consequently, menus can be developed to effortlessly navigate the portfolio, and external media and supporting files can be easily linked to any object on the slide that acts as a trigger to activate the linked files (see Figure 8–2).

Web Page Design Software

With the growing number of people interested in designing their own personal and business Web pages has come a large body of easy-to-use Web-page design software. These software packages typically require little or no programming knowledge. The programs may be used to create a digital portfolio and to place the portfolio online as a series of connected pages. A number of programs currently on the market lend themselves to portfolio design. While Web portfolio creation usually involves more technical savvy than using a priority electronic software program, Web portfolios offer the added advantages of being in a universal format that can be accessed by any computer with a browser; having a much longer life than portfolios that depend on priority software for creation and display; requiring less disk space, since most files are created in compressed formats; and providing unlimited access when published on the Web. Some of the more popular Web-page design software include:

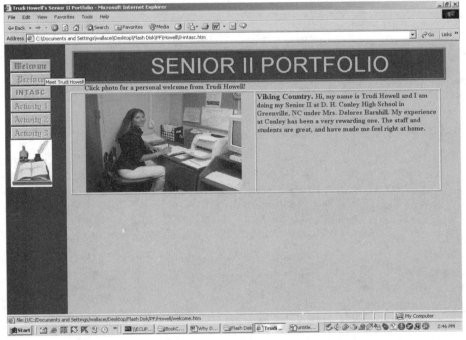

FIGURE 8–3 Example of using Web pages created in HTML format for the portfolio. The Department of Business, Career, and Technical Education students at East Carolina University designed a standard template for portfolios that can easily be navigated using the panel on the left. Then students developed individual portfolios by using the template and creating appropriate HTML, graphic, and other files that were linked into the format.

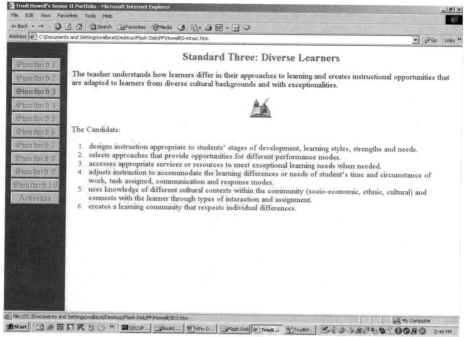

FIGURE 8-4   HTML files of INTASC standards were created and linked into the portfolios so that they would be easily viewed at any time for reference within the digital portfolio.

- Adobe PageMill 3.0 (Adobe Systems, Inc., 1999)
- Microsoft FrontPage *2002* (Microsoft Corp., 2002)
- Macromedia Dreamweaver MX *2004* (Macromedia, Inc., 2004)
- Claris Home Page 3.0 (Claris Corp.)
- Netscape Composer 7.1 (Netscape Communications Corp., 2003)

For examples of Web pages created in HTML formats for portfolios, see Figures 8–3, 8–4, 8–5, and 8–6.

Selecting Software

A number of issues should be addressed when selecting portfolio design software. These include the portfolio author's technological expertise, the portfolio design desired, and the projected audiences for the portfolio.

First, portfolio developers should carefully consider their level of technological competence. Those with less technological expertise may wish to consider using digital portfolio software that provides a template. These programs

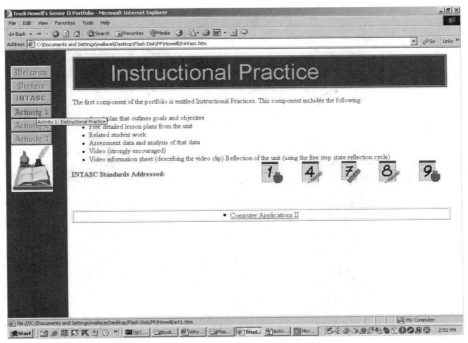

FIGURE 8–5 Example of an instructional practice unit that was developed for the HTML template showing the INTASC standards that were addressed in the Computer Applications II lesson plans in teaching the unit.

demand no real authoring skill but do run the risk of providing "cookie cutter" portfolios that all look alike. Those with more advanced technological competence may elect to use multimedia authoring programs or Web-design software.

The use of digital portfolio software packages that provide templates simplifies the design process but does so at the expense of some design originality. This may be a desirable tradeoff for the less experienced author. For those with more advanced skills and experience, multimedia packages offer greater control over the design of the digital portfolio and allow developers to create unique portfolios.

Developers should consider the audience(s) for their portfolio. Who views the portfolio, under what circumstances, and for what purposes? Placing one's portfolio online clearly offers access to the widest possible audience. Placing the portfolio on CD results in a portable portfolio, but one that must be physically delivered to the viewer. Creating a digital portfolio with extensive multimedia content requires that the viewer have access to a computer system capable of supporting the multimedia files. Consequently, there are many considerations to take into account in the development of digital portfolios.

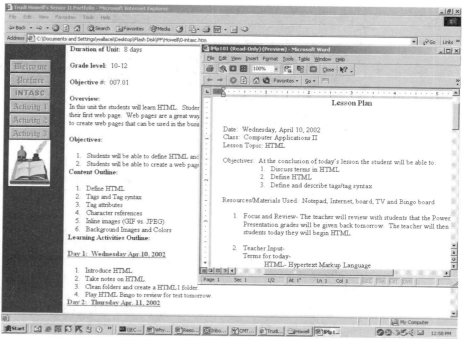

FIGURE 8–6   In this example, the overview of the eight-day lesson plan is presented with links to detailed daily lesson plans that show as the Word document in the window on the right. Within the detailed lesson plan on the right are other links to instructional activities, such as PowerPoint presentations that were developed to teach the unit and a video reflection on the unit that was presented.

HARDWARE CONSIDERATIONS

The collection and processing of entries for a digital portfolio involve using a variety of hardware. Typically, a fully equipped digital portfolio work station will include the following:

- **Computer.** Building a digital portfolio will require access to a personal computer system with adequate memory (RAM) and processing speed to support the use of multimedia software. An audio–visual computer system with video-in-and-out capability will be necessary. Since the majority of computers in operation today actually provide extremely fast processing capacity and built-in multimedia features, hardware is not an issue in most situations.
- **Scanner.** Scanners have become almost as common as printers. There are many scanners available for less than $100 that produce excellent image quality in millions of colors.
- **Digital camera.** A digital camera records images on storage media rather than film. Images captured with a digital camera may be exported directly

to a computer, manipulated and edited, and placed into a digital portfolio. Digital cameras are available in a variety of prices with an equivalent variety of features. Those with limited features can be acquired for less than $100. More sophisticated digital cameras providing greater image resolutions (1024 × 768 and higher), zoom lenses, and built-in liquid crystal display (LCD) usually cost in the $300 to $400 range. The LCD allows users to view the captured image and choose to discard or save it. The ability to immediately confirm that the captured image is the image needed for the portfolio can be of particular value in photographing fluid classroom events.

- **Video camera.** Most teachers are familiar with this technology. Media centers in most schools are equipped with a video camera that meets all the requirements for capturing video for a digital portfolio. Depending on the computer system and video camera used, it may be possible to capture video directly to the computer. In other cases, it may be necessary to transfer the video from the tape to the computer using a videocassette recorder (VCR). In either case, software is available that will allow image editing (e.g., Adobe Premier) and video compression. Compressing video is a process that results in video segments requiring much less space to store and run than uncompressed versions. In addition, streaming compressed video is recommended for Web distribution. Many video cameras today have digital storage capabilities and come with software that converts the videos into a digital file when connected to a computer. Also, many will take still digital photos and save them on smart media, flash memory, a memory stick, or other digital media so that the camera can be used in a dual role as both digital camera and video camera.
- **Writable CD-ROM drives.** In the past, limited access to a writable CD-ROM drive was a barrier to digital portfolio production. However, with the advent of technology advances in recent years, writable CD-ROM drives have become so commonplace that they are usually included as standard equipment on a computer system.

FILE FORMAT CONSIDERATIONS

From a technical standpoint, probably one of the biggest considerations in developing digital portfolios is the selection of appropriate digital file formats. Considering that most popular computer applications programs are constantly being replaced with newer versions of the products and new computer applications are being developed all the time, this creates a problem when creating a digital portfolio that can enjoy a long shelf life. When a traditional notebook-style portfolio is picked off the shelf three years from now, it will be totally intact and be pretty much the same as when it was originally created except for a little dust that accumulated on the cover. However, when a digital portfolio is picked up and inserted into the CD drive of a computer 3 years from now, there is a good chance that parts of the portfolio will not be accessible and even a good possibility that the entire portfolio cannot be accessed if careful consideration isn't give to the development of the digital portfolio. While we can usually assume that the media itself will be somewhat stable, consider that there is a constant evolution in computer hardware, and components tend to get smaller with higher capacities on a regular basis. Consequently, just as the 8-inch floppy disk gave way to 5.25-inch floppy disks, which then gave way to 3.5-inch floppy disks—now almost extinct—it is a gamble to know what storage method will be the medium of choice 3 years from now. Already, 3" CDs are starting to replace 4.75-inch CDs, so in the future there may not be a CD player around that can even accept the standard-sized CD used today. High-capacity Zip disks have already become practically extinct, so on what storage medium should the digital portfolio be saved to enjoy as long a shelf life as possible?

It is important to know that digital data can be changed from one format to another quite easily. All files should be converted into their most universal generic form so that they at least stand a chance of being useable in the future. For example, most text documents today are created with a word processor and saved in a format that is unique to the particular word processor being used to create the file. While it would be quite easy to link actual word processing files to a portfolio, it might work and be effective if the user has the same particular word processor and version loaded on his or her computer. But if he or she does not have the correct word processor, the file may be entirely useless. For example, Microsoft Word XP, which is the word processor of choice today, saves in a format called .doc, meaning "document." However, if a portfolio viewer does not have Word XP or has an older version of Word, the file may not be opened. Since most word processors also save in a format called Rich Text Format (RTF), it would be wiser to save the files in RTF format than .doc, since RTF is more universal. Better yet, why not save the file in HTML format, since nearly every computer today is Internet ready and HTML is the universal text-file format used on the Internet? Another possibility would be to convert all text files to Acrobat PDF format, which retains all of the formatting of the original document and displays it the same way on all computers. However, the Acrobat converter is an extra software package that would need to be purchased.

The most universal formats that exist today were designed for the Web. Consequently, a good rule of thumb would be to put all files in formats that are used on the Internet and don't require additional players or plug-ins to be viewed or played.

CONCERNS ASSOCIATED WITH DESIGNING A DIGITAL PORTFOLIO

Portfolio developers must consider a number of issues before deciding to design a digital portfolio. As exciting and promising as this emerging technology may be, some barriers prevent its widespread use.

Not all digital portfolios can be viewed on all computer platforms. Some digital portfolio software is platform specific. Some portfolio viewers may use computer systems not capable of supporting the multimedia content that is used in digital portfolios. While it seems likely that this issue will become less significant as more people have and use multimedia-capable computer systems, at the present time it is a legitimate concern.

Designing a digital portfolio may require substantial time and effort devoted to mastering the requisite technologies. Portfolio developers who have little experience with the hardware and software necessary to develop digital portfolios and who have little time to devote to mastering these technologies may find a traditional format more efficient. This will become less of an issue as more professionals feel comfortable with technology.

Designing a digital portfolio requires access to a variety of hardware and software. While most schools have these technologies on hand, many individuals may not. Even in school settings, the absence of enough equipment to assure quick and easy access may be an issue complicating digital portfolio design and frustrating portfolio developers.

In addition, if digital portfolios are going to be capable of being viewed by wider audiences via the Internet, privacy and legal issues must be considered for materials made available on the Web. Consequently, consent forms and other waivers need to be obtained from students providing permission for their materials to be made available to audiences through Web access. Identification and password protection may be necessary to protect the material from open scrutiny on the entire World Wide Web.

There is the possibility that developers or viewers of digital portfolios may find themselves focusing on the design and presentation technologies rather than on the content of the portfolio. Digital portfolios have value only to the extent that the content is carefully chosen, effectively organized, and rationally interpreted. Placing a poor portfolio into digital format does not improve the quality of its content.

CLOSING THOUGHTS

Digital portfolios represent a powerful and innovative medium for the development and presentation of teaching portfolios. The hardware and software required for constructing digital portfolios are commonly available in most school and university settings. Prospective and current teachers should possess the technological skills necessary to use the hardware and software. Portfolios are becoming a more common means of documenting and presenting evidence of teaching competence. In the future, the digital portfolio may become the preferred way of designing, constructing, storing, transporting, and presenting teaching portfolios.

CHAPTER ACTIVITIES

Activity 1—Creating a 2-Minute Video Reflection

This activity is designed to give you experience in creating a video reflection that can be included in a digital portfolio. Most Web cameras come with software that creates .avi files. Your objective is to create a professional video reflection in the .avi format. If your camera and software produces other formats, that will be fine. You may have to make several attempts at this, since "practice makes perfect." You may do this "off the top of your head," or, if you are more comfortable with a written script, you may prepare one first. Using a Web camera attached to a personal computer, set the capture size to 320 × 240. Make sure your microphone is attached and working properly if it is not built into the camera or the computer.

Look directly into the camera, making sure that you are centered in the capture area, and then present a 2-minute reflection of your philosophy of teaching. If you want to use another topic for your reflection, examine the reflection chapter in this book for possible topics and use one of them instead of this suggested topic. After you have completed your video, play it back and review it, checking for the following:

1. Is your audio level loud and clear without any hissing or background noise?
2. Are you enunciating and speaking with adequate voice inflection?
3. Is your picture centered in the video area?
4. Are you looking directly into the camera as though you are speaking to another person?
5. Are you smiling and pleasant?
6. Do you appear to be relaxed and at ease?
7. Is the lighting adequate to make an attractive video?
8. Did your video length come within 10 seconds of the 2-minute time period?
9. If you are using a script, does it appear that you are reading?
10. Are there excessive head and body movements?
11. Is there excessive blinking of your eyes?

If you answered yes to questions 1–8 and no to 9–11, you probably have a very acceptable video. If your video is not acceptable after you have reviewed it, make as many attempts as possible until you have achieved a professional video reflection. After you are satisfied with the results of your video reflection, use the "Save As" command and save the file as "MyVideo." *(Do not attempt to save the video on a floppy diskette, since the file will be much too large to fit on one.)*

Activity 2—Creating Exhibits from Screen Images

This activity is designed to give you experience in creating screen shots, or "digital snapshots," that can be included in a digital portfolio to demonstrate technological competencies. Your objective is to create three graphic files that show a sample of your technological work by first having the work visible on your computer screen and then taking a screen shot and saving it as a graphic file in JPEG format. Exhibits showing a word processed document, an electronic grade book, a multimedia presentation, or a tutorial program being used in a class are examples of what you can include. Follow these steps to create a screen shot:

1. Open the file or program, and display on your screen the contents that you want to capture.
2. Maximize the window that the file is in so that you can get as much of it as possible visible on your screen.

Student Name	Photo (Assignment)	Audio (Assignment)	Paint (Assignment)	Draw (Assignment)	Flyer (Assignment)	Tri (Assignment)	Five (Assignment)	DTP (Other)	PPT15 (Other)	HTML (Assignment)	Terms (Assignment)	Web Project (Other)	ASIP 5200 Midterm (Quiz)	5200 Final Summer 02 (Quiz)	Total Points	Total Weighted Score
Bas	90	100	100	100	95	86	100	84	75	90	100	92	76	94	1282	87.74
Bes	100	100	100	100	95	93	95	90	93	90	100	94	84	88	1322	92.14
Bos	90	100	100	100	95	85	95	88	86	80	100	84	79	90	1272	88.08
Bro	100	100	100	100	95	97	95	89	88	90	66	96	81	81	1278	89.28
Cor	100	100	100	100	92	95	100	94	95	100	100	96	90	85	1347	93.54
Cou	100	100	100	100	100	100	100	93	100	100	100	98	90	100	1381	98
Doz	100	100	100	90	93	95	96	91	90	100	100	83	74	88	1300	89.36
Fra	100	100	100	85	-	-	92	92	91	90	66	73	88	88	1065	83.22
Gilb	100	100	80	100	100	90	95	98	92	80	100	90	82	89	1296	92.34
Joh	100	80	100	90	95	92	95	80	70	90	100	71	71	69	1203	76.26
Jon	100	100	100	85	100	96	95	95	96	90	100	98	69	91	1330	95
Kal	100	100	80	100	96	95	100	98	92	90	100	98	91	92	1352	95.44
Lup	100	100	100	100	100	88	93	95	95	100	100	97	93	90	1351	94.88
Mcl	80	0	90	78	95	90	95	82	68	100	100	64	65	52	1081	69.5
Mcl	90	100	100	95	100	90	100	87	58	70	33	83	74	91	1176	80.94
Mye	100	100	89	100	100	85	100	88	83	80	100	71	84	77	1268	82.78
Par	80	90	100	100	100	95	90	100	80	80	0	93	86	84	1178	84.22
Qur	100	100	100	100	98	97	100	93	64	100	100	66	86	74	1278	79.02

FIGURE 8–7   In this example of Creating Exhibits from Screen Images, the student positions the Excel gradebook on the computer screen and presses "Print Screen" to take a digital snapshot of the spreadsheet. The resulting image can be pasted directly into PowerPoint or pasted into Microsoft Paint and then saved as an image file to be used in an HTML document.

continued...

3. If you are using a program that allows you to zoom in or out, zoom in or out as necessary to put as much emphasis on the area of your document that you intend to show.

4. Use your vertical and horizontal scroll bars to position your work so that it optimizes the area that you want to capture. Press the "Print Screen" button on your keyboard to capture the screen image. This places your screen shot on your clipboard so that it can be pasted into another.

5. If you are using PowerPoint to create a digital portfolio, you may now paste your screen-captured image onto a slide.

6. If you need to edit your captured image, you may now open Windows Paint or any other image editing software that you have access to and paste your image in the editor.

7. Crop the image as necessary to cut out any unnecessary part of the image that may detract from the focus of your screen shot. (Carefully consider what you crop if you choose to do so, since showing the document within the window of an actual application such as Word or Excel may actually enhance the exhibit that you are attempting to portray.)

8. Now using the "Save As" command, save the file as "MySnap01" in a JPEG format. (Your Paint software will have options as to what format you want to save in.)

9. Continue this process to complete the digital exhibits that could be included in a digital portfolio and capture two more screens and save them as "MySnap02" and "MySnap03."

Activity 3—Creating Exhibits from Scanned Images

This activity is designed to give you experience in creating scanning evidence that can be included in a digital portfolio. Your objective is to create three graphic files that show a sample of your technology work by scanning the images and saving them as graphic files in a JPEG or GIF format. Examples of what you can do would include showing a sample of a quiz or exam on which you have made handwritten comments, a handwritten note from a parent, or any other handwritten document that you want to include as evidence. The process is as follows:

1. Make sure your scanner is plugged in and properly connected to your computer.

2. Make sure your computer is operating correctly and has the scanning software installed and working properly.

3. If you are using a flatbed scanner, position your document squarely onto the scanner surface.

4. If you are using a sheet-fed scanner, feed the document into the scanner, making sure it is straight within the scanner guides.

5. Launch the scanner software and set it for "Image."

continued...

6. If your document has color, set the software to capture color. Otherwise set it for black-and-white.
7. If your scanner provides a preview, use your "Select Tool" and draw a box around the area of the document you want scanned.
8. Scan the document and, using the "Save As" command, save the file as "MyScan01" in a JPEG format if it is a color document, or in a GIF format if your document is black-and-white. (Your scanning software will have options as to the format in which you want to save the document.)
9. Continue this process, capturing two more documents and saving them as "MyScan02" and "MyScan03."
10. Open your files with Microsoft Paint or any other image editing software you may have available and examine your scanned files. If they look visually acceptable, simply close them and they will be ready to use. However, you may need to crop the image, change the contrast, or touch it up a bit. If that is the case, manipulate the image with your image editing software as necessary and then save the edited file.

REFERENCES

Adobe Systems, Inc. (1999). Adobe PageMill 3.0 [Computer software]. San Jose, CA: Author.

Baron, C. (1996). *Creating a digitial portfolio.* Indianapolis, IN: Hayden Books.

Guenter, C. (1998). *Student teaching electronic portfolio.* Chico, CA: California State University, Department of Education.

Ivers, K. S., & Barron, A. E. (1998). *Multimedia projects in education: Designing, producing, and assessing.*

Lankes, A. M. (1995). Electronic portfolios: A new idea in assessment [Electronic version, EDO-IR-95-9]. *ERIC Digest, 95*(9), 1–4. Abstract retrieved from Clearinghouse on Information and Technology Web site: http://ericir.syr.edu/ithome/digests/portfolio.html

Macromedia, Inc. (2004). Macromedia Dreamweaver MX 2004 [Computer software]. San Francisco: Author.

Microsoft Corp. (2002). Microsoft FrontPage 2002 [Computer software]. Redmond, WA: Author.

Netscape Communications Corp. (2003). Netscape Composer 7.1 [Computer software]. Mountain View, CA: Author.

Perone, V. (Ed.). (1991). *Expanding student assessment.* Alexandria, VA: Association of Supervision and Curriculum Development.

Scholastic, Inc. (1995). Scholastic Electronic Portfolio [Computer software]. New York: Author.

Watts, M. M. (1997). Technology as catalyst. *Educational Perspectives: Journal of the College of Education/University of Hawaii at Manoa, 31*(2), 28–31.

Webster University, School of Education. (2004). *Electronic professional portfolios for teachers.* Retrieved April 17, 2004, from http://owl.webster.edu/eportfolio/resources.html

Reflection Analyses for Chapter 3

AUTHOR'S ANALYSIS FOR REFLECTION 1

Score: ++ This reflection is excellent. It gives an excellent description, analysis, and planning for future teaching. The description is clear. The audience is a university professor, and the student writes in first person, appropriate for a self-reflection. In the analysis section, the student honestly looks at her strengths and weaknesses in relation to planning and delivering this lesson. The analysis is the strongest part of the reflection.

AUTHOR'S ANALYSIS FOR REFLECTION 2

Score: + This reflection is well done. It is clearly written and gives a good description and analysis of the lesson. In addition, planning for future teaching was highlighted. In comparison to the first reflection in Chapter 3, this example does not give the extent of detail or the depth of analysis but meets all of the criteria appropriate for reflection.

AUTHOR'S ANALYSIS FOR REFLECTION 3

Score: +/− The writer provided a mediocre description (sometimes off the subject), but wrote a good analysis and did a good job on future impact. The description did not contain enough details for a reader to form an accurate picture of the evidence. In addition, the writing is not clear and there are many grammatical and spelling errors. A peer reader would have been helpful in this case.

Sample Portfolio Guides for Beginning Teachers to Obtain Licensure: North Carolina and Connecticut

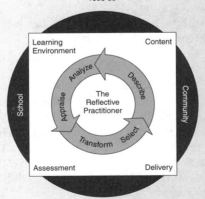

Performance-Based
Licensure
1998-99

Three Years of Guided,
Professional Growth for New Teachers

 Public Schools of North Carolina
State Board of Education
Department of Public Instruction

Used by permission of Public Schools of North Carolina, State
Board of Education, Department of Public Instruction

ACTIVITY 1 DEMONSTRATING YOUR CONTENT KNOWLEDGE AND ABILITY TO TEACH IT

Standards to Be Addressed: 1, 2, 4, 6, 7, 8

Required:
Coordinated set of evidence

Components:

- Unit plan and goals (labeled clearly)
- 5 contiguous lesson plans (with dates)
- Related student work and assessment and test data
- Analysis of student achievement data
- Video for Activity 1
- Video information sheet
- Reflection

Optional:
Related evidence and artifacts
In this activity, the candidate is expected to demonstrate that he or she:

- Has an understanding of the central concepts of his or her discipline
- Uses explanations and representations that link curriculum to prior learning
- Uses interdisciplinary approaches to teaching and learning
- Uses methods of inquiry that are central to the discipline
- Provides opportunities for students to assume responsibility for and be actively engaged in their learning
- Encourages student reflection on prior knowledge and its connection to new information
- Accesses student thinking as a basis for instructional activities through group and individual interaction and written work (listening, encouraging discussion, eliciting samples of student thinking orally and in writing)
- Selects and uses multiple teaching and learning strategies (a variety of presentations and explanations) to encourage students in critical thinking and problem solving
- Encourages students to assume responsibility for identifying and using learning resources
- Assumes different roles in the instructional process (instructor, facilitator, coach, audience) to accommodate content, purpose, and learner needs
- Models effective communication strategies in conveying ideas and information and when asking questions (e.g., monitoring the effects of messages; restating ideas and drawing connections; using visual, aural, and kinesthetic cues; being sensitive to nonverbal cues both given and received)

- Provides support for learner expression in speaking, writing, and other media
- Uses a variety of media communication tools to enrich learning opportunities
- Develops plans that are appropriate for curriculum goals and are based on effective instruction
- Adjusts plans to respond to unanticipated sources of input or student needs
- Develops short- and long-range plans
- Selects, constructs, and uses assessment strategies appropriate to learning outcomes
- Uses a variety of informal and formal strategies to determine student progress and to adjust instruction (e.g., standardized test data; peer and student self-assessment; and informal assessments such as observations, surveys, interviews, student work, performance tasks, portfolios, and teacher-made tests)
- Evaluates the effects of class activities on individuals and on groups through observation of classroom interaction, questioning, and analysis of student work

Directions to the Candidate

1. Select a concept from the *North Carolina Standard Course of Study* or other state-adopted curriculum documents appropriate to your field.
2. Collect and compile the required evidence related to that concept and any additional evidence you want to use to support the standards addressed.
3. Describe how you taught this concept in terms of instructional planning, resources, delivery, and assessment.
4. Address how your assessment and test data affected your instructional planning and delivery.
5. Use the questions on the following page to guide your reflection.

WRITING THE REFLECTION

Below are the guiding questions for the required reflection for Activity 1. In an effort to tailor your product to your style, you may choose to follow the questions exactly as they are posed, use them strictly as an outline for topics that need to be covered as you reflect, or use the indicators from the INTASC standards addressed in Activity 1 for writing your reflection. Note: The questions come directly from those indicators. Again, choose your evidence or artifacts carefully; they should show your development as a professional as well as their impact on your students. Be sure that your reflection references the evidence or artifacts that you have included with Activity 1.

Select

1. What concept are you addressing from your content area?
2. Why did you decide to address this concept?
3. How does this concept relate to your students' age group?

Describe

1. Briefly describe the demographics of your class(es). Include a breakdown by gender, race, grade levels, and other characteristics. Include a description of any particular student needs in the classroom.
2. What unique student characteristics did you consider in planning the lessons?
3. What diverse student perspectives did you consider in planning the lessons?
4. What kind of assessment of student learning and development did you use prior to planning the lesson(s)? How did you identify exceptional learning needs?
5. Did the school (district) have appropriate resources or materials for this unit? What materials or resources did you choose to use? Include any media tools you incorporated.
6. What resources or services did you incorporate in this unit?
7. What kinds of multiple teaching strategies did you choose to incorporate in your lesson(s)?
8. What roles (coach, audience, facilitator, etc.) did you play to encourage student learning?
9. What strategies did you use to assess student learning? What assessments are required?
10. How did you maintain records of student work and performance?

Analyze

1. How did your assessment of prior student learning and development influence the lesson design?
2. How did the unique characteristics (including exceptional learning needs) of your students impact your planning for the unit?
3. How did you allow students to use different performance modes (writing, speaking, behaving, etc.)?
4. How did you link your students' experiences with the events and experiences of this lesson(s)?
5. How did your plan(s) allow modification for unanticipated sources of input or unanticipated student needs?
6. How did you evaluate the available resources or materials for inclusion in the lesson(s)?
7. Why did you select the teaching and assessment strategies you incorporated in the lesson?

8. How did you:
    * Demonstrate a link to students' prior learning?
    * Show the use of a variety of informal and formal assessment strategies to inform choices and adjust instruction?
    * Show that you have addressed long- and short-range planning based on your knowledge of the subject matter, students, community, and curriculum goals?
9. How does the video show your support for learner expression?
10. How have you taken gender and culture into account in your communication with students?

Appraise

1. What new learning resulted from the activity(ies) conducted for you and your students?
2. How did the use of selected multiple teaching strategies increase your students' opportunities to engage in critical thinking and problem-solving activities?
3. How effectively were you able to use the available resources or materials for this lesson?
4. Which media communication tools have been most and least effective in your classroom?
5. How successful was the lesson? What aspect was most effective? Least effective?

Transform

1. What did you learn from planning the lesson?
2. How did you adjust instruction as a result of assessment of student learning?
3. In teaching this unit or a similar unit in the future, how will this experience influence your choice of instructional and assessment techniques?
4. What did you learn from the selection of multiple teaching strategies?

ACTIVITY 2 EXAMINING THE SCHOOL–COMMUNITY LINK: YOUR ROLE IN A LEARNING COMMUNITY

Standard to be Addressed: 10

Required:

* Professional contribution log
* Parent–guardian communication log

Components:

- Parent survey(s) example and summary
- Reflection

Optional:

Related evidence and artifacts
In this activity, the candidate is expected to demonstrate that she or he:

- Participates in collegial activities designed to make the entire school a productive learning environment
- Links with counselors, teachers of other classes and activities within the school, professionals in community agencies, and others in the community to support students' learning and well-being
- Seeks to establish cooperative partnerships with parents and guardians to support student learning
- Advocates for students

Directions to the Candidate

1. Collect and compile the required evidence as well as any additional evidence you want to use to support the standard addressed.
2. Create a parent survey or use the sample parent survey in the Tool Kit.
3. Summarize the findings of your parent survey. You will need to create a form that details the number of responses to each question as well as provides the anecdotal comments from the parents surveyed. If you create your own survey, include a copy.
4. Use the following questions to guide your reflection.

WRITING THE REFLECTION

Below are the guiding questions for the required reflection for Activity 2. In an effort to tailor your product to your style, you may choose to follow the questions exactly as they are posed, use them strictly as an outline for topics which need to be covered as you reflect, or use the indicators from INTASC Standard 10 addressed in Activity 2 for writing your reflection. Note: The questions come directly from those indicators. Again, choose your evidence/artifacts carefully; they should show your development as a professional as well as their impact on your students. Be sure that your reflection references the evidence and artifacts you have included with Activity 2.

Select

1. How do the evidence and artifacts you have selected address Standard 10?

Describe

1. In what collegial activities did you participate to make the entire school a productive learning environment?
2. What partnerships did you establish with the parents or guardians of your students?
3. What interactions did you maintain with counselors, other teachers, community agencies, and others to support students' well-being?

Analyze

1. How and for what reasons did you establish partnerships with parents and guardians? Refer to the evidence presented in your product.
2. How does the evidence presented show your advocacy for students?
3. How did the activities presented allow you to participate in making the entire school a productive learning environment?
4. Based on the information from your parent surveys, what are some positive and negative steps that you have taken this year related to parent and student contact?

Appraise

1. What benefits have been derived from the partnerships you have established with parents, guardians, and others in the school community?

Transform

1. Based on your experiences, what strategies will you use in the future to establish your role as a learner and advocate in the school community?

ACTIVITY 3 FOCUSING ON THE CLASSROOM CLIMATE

Standard to be Addressed: 5

Required:

- Classroom management plan
- Comparison of discipline rates

Components:

- Video for Activity 3
- Video information sheet
- Reflection

Optional:

Related evidence and artifacts

In this activity, the candidate is expected to demonstrate that she or he:

- Encourages clear procedures and expectations that ensure students assume responsibility for themselves and others, work collaboratively and independently, and engage in purposeful learning activities
- Engages students by relating lessons to students' personal interests, allowing students to have choices in their learning, and leading students to ask questions and solve problems that are meaningful to them
- Organizes, allocates, and manages time, space, and activities in a way that is conducive to learning
- Organizes, prepares students for, and monitors independent and group work that allows for the full and varied participation of all individuals
- Analyzes classroom environment and interactions and makes adjustments to enhance social relationships, student motivation and engagement, and productive work

Directions to the Candidate

1. Include a copy of your classroom management plan that is clearly labeled.
2. Collect and compile evidence or artifacts you want to use to support Standard 5.
3. Summarize your student surveys, if you wish.
4. Use the following questions to guide your reflection.

WRITING THE REFLECTION

Below are the guiding questions for the required reflection for Activity 3. In an effort to tailor your product to your style, you may choose to follow the questions exactly as they are posed, use them strictly as an outline for topics that need to be covered as you reflect, or use the indicators from INTASC Standard 5 addressed in Activity 3 for writing your reflection. Note: The questions come directly from those indicators. Again, choose your evidence and artifacts carefully; they should show your development as a professional as well as their impact on your students. Be sure that your reflection references the evidence and artifacts that you have included with Activity 3.

Select

1. What evidence and artifacts have you selected to address Standard 5?

Describe

1. Describe your classroom management plan. What guidelines did you use to develop it?

2. Describe a student who was a discipline challenge during the year. In reflecting on the situation, what specific actions did you take that were productive? What specific actions did you take that were unproductive?
3. What interactions did you maintain with counselors, other teachers, community agencies, and others to support students' well-being?

Analyze

1. Describe three adjustments in your classroom environment that you have made to ensure that students are engaged in learning rather than in inappropriate behavior.
2. How do you manage time, space, and activities to ensure that students are actively engaged in learning?
3. When did you develop your classroom management plan? What have you done to implement it? Have you modified it? If so, how?
4. How do you provide relevance and choice to engage students in their own learning?

Appraise

1. Explain how the evidence presented (management plan, video, etc.) shows that you have established clear procedures and expectations that students will assume responsibility for themselves and others, work collaboratively and independently, and engage in purposeful learning activities.

Transform

1. What kind of adjustments have you made to your management plan, and what was the impact of those changes?
2. Based on your experiences, what changes might you make in your management plan in the future?

ACTIVITY 4 ADDRESSING STUDENTS' UNIQUE LEARNING NEEDS

Standards to be Addressed: 2, 3, 8, 10

Required:

- Two case studies

Components:

- Related student work
- Student test or assessment data

- Video for Activity 4
- Video information sheet
- Reflection

Optional:

Related evidence or artifacts

In this activity, the candidate is expected to demonstrate that she or he:

- Evaluates student performance to design instruction appropriate for social, cognitive, and emotional development
- Designs instruction appropriate to students' stages of development, learning styles, strengths, and needs
- Creates relevance for students by linking with their prior experiences
- Selects approaches that provide opportunities for different performance modes
- Accesses appropriate services or resources to meet exceptional learning needs
- Adjusts instruction to accommodate the learning differences or needs of students (time and circumstance of work, tasks assigned, communication, and response modes)
- Plans lessons and activities to address variations in learning styles and performance modes, multiple developmental levels of diverse learners, and problem solving and exploration
- Uses knowledge of different cultural contexts within the community (socioeconomic, ethnic, cultural) and connects with the learner through types of interaction and assignments
- Creates a learning community that respects individual differences
- Maintains useful records of student work and performance and can communicate student progress knowledgeably and responsibly
- Links with counselors, teachers of other classes and activities within the school, professionals in community agencies, and others in the community to support students' learning and well-being

Directions to the Candidate

1. From the case studies that you have done during the school term (quarter, semester, year, or other length of student interaction), choose two students with different physical, social, emotional, and intellectual characteristics that have affected their learning. In choosing the students, remember that you need to show student growth as facilitated by your actions and interactions.
2. Write case studies of these students that include, but are not limited to: the particular learning problems of the students; the instructional strategies that you have used or modified to improve their learning; the changes you have noted in the students since you began your interactions; other factors that have affected their learning and the level

of success of your interventions; and the types of records you have kept related to these students. Your case studies should be no more than one page each.

3. Provide examples of modified student work related to the coordinated set of lesson plans in Activity 1 for the students in the case studies as well as for other students with particular needs.

4. Collect and compile any additional evidence you want to use to support the standards addressed.

5. Realize that some of the questions in the reflection will refer to the lesson plans that you included in Activity 1.

6. Summarize student surveys, if you wish.

7. Use the questions on the following page to guide your reflection.

WRITING THE REFLECTION

Below are the guiding questions for the required reflection for Activity 4. In an effort to tailor your product to your style, you may choose to follow the questions exactly as they are posed, use them strictly as an outline for topics that need to be covered as you reflect, or use the indicators from the INTASC standards addressed in Activity 4 for writing your reflection. Note: The questions come directly from those indicators. Again, choose your evidence or artifacts carefully; they should show your development as a professional as well as their impact on your students. Be sure that your reflection references the evidence and artifacts that you have included with Activity 4.

Select

1. What evidence and artifacts have you selected to address the INTASC standards?

Describe

1. What are the unique characteristics that distinguish these students from others (learning styles, prior experiences, exceptional needs, background, etc.)?

2. What steps did you take to assess the needs of these students?

3. With whom and in what ways did you communicate the needs and progress of these students?

4. From whom and in what ways did you solicit information about the students' experiences, learning behaviors, needs, and progress?

Analyze

1. How did your assessment of the characteristics and needs of these students affect your planning instruction and interactions with them?

2. As you implemented your lesson plans, what adjustments did you make to accommodate the learning differences or needs of these students as well as the variety of students in your whole class? In other words, how did you meet all of your students' needs?
3. What evidence or artifacts have you provided that show you met the needs of a variety of students?
4. How did the cultural context of these students influence your planning for them and your interactions with them?
5. How did you incorporate cultural knowledge into your lesson plans?
6. How did you select and incorporate special resources or services for these students?

Appraise

1. What interventions or interactions with these students were productive in improving student learning or behavior?
2. What interventions or interactions with these students were unproductive in improving student learning or behavior?
3. What sources of information and assistance were most helpful to you in meeting the unique needs of these students?
4. Were the students identified in your case studies successful this year? Why or why not?

Transform

1. By developing the case studies, what did you learn about the diverse nature and needs of students?
2. What new learning on your part will you incorporate in your future teaching?

ACTIVITY 5 APPRAISING YOURSELF AS A PROFESSIONAL

Standard to be Addressed: 9

Required:

- Beginning teacher individualized growth plan

Components:

- Self-administered interview (clearly labeled)
  Year 1
  Year 2
  Year 3 (if applicable)

- Summative evaluation
  Year 1
  Year 2
  Year 3 (if applicable)
- Reflection (Note: The required reflection from each activity in the product will also be used to assess this activity.)

Optional:

Related evidence and artifacts
The candidate is expected to demonstrate that she or he:

- Uses classroom observation, information about students, and research as sources for evaluating the outcomes of teaching and learning and as a basis for experimenting with, reflecting on, and revising practice
- Uses professional literature, colleagues, and other resources (such as professional organizations) to support self-development as a learner and as a teacher
- Consults with colleagues within the school and in other professional arenas to gather support for writing a reflection, problem solving, generating new ideas, actively sharing experiences, and seeking and giving feedback

Directions to the Candidate

1. Complete the Beginning Teacher Individualized Growth Plan at the end of Year 1, Year 2, and Year 3, if applicable.
2. Collect and compile any additional evidence you want to use to support Standard 9.
3. Include up to three colleagues' surveys, if you wish.

A Guide to the Best Program for Beginning Teachers 2003–2004

THE BEGINNING EDUCATOR
SUPPORT AND TRAINING
PROGRAM

The Beginning Educator Support and Training Program

Connecticut State Department of Education
Bureau of Educator Assessment
P.O. Box 2219
Hartford, Connecticut 06145

A Guide to the Best Program for Beginning Teachers
2003–2004

TABLE OF CONTENTS

CHAPTER 3: THE BEST PROGRAM PORTFOLIO ASSESSMENT

Beginning teachers first registered in the BEST Program during the 2003–2004 school year who are teaching and are certified in the areas of bilingual education, elementary education, English language arts, mathematics, middle grades, physical education, science, social studies, special education, visual arts and world languages, must successfully complete the portfolio assessment as a participation requirement in the BEST Program.

This chapter describes the BEST Program portfolio assessment process, of which successful completion is required for beginning teachers who are participating in the **Portfolio Induction Program.**

The sections in this chapter include:

Section A: Special Notice Regarding Participation of Elementary/Middle Grades Certified Teachers

Section B: The BEST Program Portfolio Assessment

Section C: Scoring of the Portfolio Assessment

Section D: Portfolio Performance Standards and Score Descriptions

Section E: Portfolio Completion Standard

Section F: Code of Professional Responsibility

Section G: Important Notice about Third Year Participation

Section H: Submission of Portfolio in Year One

Section I: Change in Teaching Assignment from Year One to Year Two

Section J: Documentation of Special Circumstances

Section K: Exemption Policy for the BEST Portfolio Assessment

Section L: Science Safety Self-Assessment (science teachers only)

Section A: Special Notice Regarding Participation of Elementary and Middle Grades Certified Teachers

1. *Elementary certified teachers:*

   - Beginning teachers, who *teach multiple subjects in a self-contained classroom,* should participate in the elementary component of the Portfolio Induction Program.

   - *Elementary certified teachers* whose teaching assignment is English-language arts only (including integrated language arts, developmental reading, remedial reading/language arts), or mathematics only (including remedial mathematics) may petition through the portfolio exemption process to complete *only the literacy* or *only the numeracy* portion of the elementary portfolio. *Note that a petition for exemption from either the literacy or numeracy portion of the portfolio will not be considered until year two of participation in BEST. (See page 29 for more information on the exemption process.)*

   - *Elementary certified teachers* who teach social studies only or science only, or a combination of both, are required to complete a social studies or science portfolio.

2. *Middle school certified teachers:*

   - Beginning middle school certified teachers who teach primarily one subject area (such as English/language arts, history/social studies, mathematics or science) should participate in the component of the Portfolio Induction Program that corresponds to their primary teaching assignment, by submitting a portfolio in that content area. If a middle grades teacher is assigned to teach more than one subject area, he or she should select the BEST participation area that corresponds to his or her primary teaching assignment (representing his or her greater course load).

Section B: The BEST Program Portfolio Assessment

The BEST Program teacher portfolio assessments have been designed to assess the foundational skills and competencies as well as discipline-specific teaching standards identified in *Connecticut's Common Core of Teaching* (see **Appendix 10**).

All portfolios, regardless of the content area, require the following documentation:

- daily lesson plans for a 5–8 hour unit of instruction with one class;

- two or three videotaped segments of teaching equaling in total approximately 40 minutes;

- examples of the work of two students; and

- reflective commentaries on teaching and learning that took place during the unit.

In summary, the teacher generally writes about **12–16** pages of commentaries plus completes 5–8 lesson logs, depending upon the length of the unit. The remainder of the portfolio consists of copies of instructional materials and examples of student work and the videotape.

Portfolio handbooks in each disciplinary area provide information about the specific requirements of the portfolio. Portfolio handbooks will be made available on a CD-Rom and distributed by mail to school addresses of all first and second year teachers. In addition, portfolio handbooks are available through the *"BEST Connections"* website at www.ctbest.org, click on *BEST Resource Documents.* Annually, a committee of beginning and experienced teachers is convened to review the portfolio handbooks to ensure clarity of tasks and questions, review page limits and ensure that there is no redundancy of information requested in the portfolio.

Feedback on your portfolio: All beginning teachers receive an **individualized performance summary,** which describes their performance in the categories of designing and implementing instruction, assessment of learning, and analysis of teaching. All beginning teachers who do not successfully complete the portfolio assessment are encouraged to schedule a **BEST Portfolio Assessment Conference (PAC).** During such conferences, a trained portfolio scorer/trainer meets individually with a beginning teacher to help him/her interpret the score report and discuss strategies for improvement.

Where Can I Go for Help?

- **BEST Connections, which provides BEST information, communication and registration at website** www.ctbest.org has been set up to ensure that all BEST Program participants receive ongoing communications from BEST Program staff, portfolio project leaders, and teachers-in-residence. To receive ongoing communications through your e-mail, go to www.ctbest.org, **and sign-up for electronic communications.**

- **General information** about the BEST Program and the portfolio assessment can be found on the *BEST Connections* website at www.ctbest.org, click on BEST Resource Documents. These resources include: *A Guide to the BEST Program for Beginning Teachers, Portfolio Handbooks in ten subject areas, all portfolio-related forms, Portfolio Feedback Rubrics, Seminars in ten subject areas and the Common Core of Teaching.*

- **BEST Connections** is also a registration site for all BEST Professional Development seminars for beginning teachers. To view all professional development offerings for beginning teachers go to www.ctbest.org.

- **BEST Portfolio exemplars** are made available at each RESC for viewing by beginning teachers and their mentors. These examples represent a selection of beginning teacher portfolios in each content area. To view these exemplars, call your nearest RESC to schedule an appointment (see Appendix 4 for a list of the RESCs). Some districts have purchased copies of portfolio exemplars (check with your district facilitator). In addition, the "online" discipline-specific seminars contain a sample portfolio for each of the respective disciplines (see website address above).

- **Support of Colleagues:** In addition to your mentor, seek out others who have completed BEST portfolios and those that are trained portfolio scorers.

Section C: Scoring of the Portfolio Assessment

The BEST teaching portfolios submitted during a beginning teacher's second year of participation in BEST are scored during the following summer. Portfolios are evaluated by experienced educators with extensive teaching experience in the same disciplinary area as the beginning teacher. Each assessor has participated in at least 50 hours of comprehensive training in the scoring of teaching portfolios and each has demonstrated reliability in scoring. Any portfolio that does not meet the acceptable performance standard is rescored independently by additional portfolio scorers to confirm the rating.

The portfolio evaluation process, which takes approximately 4–5 hours per portfolio, consists of four steps:

Collecting and recording evidence through note taking: Assessors carefully review all components of the portfolio and take detailed notes.

Interpreting the evidence: Evidence is then organized around a series of **guiding questions and performance indicators,** which are derived from the discipline-specific professional teaching standards. The portfolio handbooks include a list of these guiding questions so that beginning teachers are fully aware of the criteria by which their portfolios will be evaluated.

Evaluating the quality of the teaching documented in the portfolio: Assessors then identify patterns of evidence that lead to a final overall score.

Providing data for the portfolio score report: Each beginning teacher receives an individual portfolio performance profile and feedback rubric, which summarizes a beginning teacher's performance on the portfolio. This report is sent to beginning teachers in early September. To view a sample score report, go to www.ctbest.org, click on *"BEST Resource Documents"* and scroll down to "Portfolio Performance Feedback Rubrics."

Section D: Portfolio Performance Standards and Score Descriptions for Teachers of Elementary, English Language Arts, Mathematics, Music, Physical Education, Science, Social Studies, Special Education and Visual Arts

On June 2, 2000, the State Board of Education established standards for the evaluation of BEST teaching portfolios. The standards are based upon the foundational skills and competencies of the CCT related to teacher knowledge, planning, instruction and assessment as well as the discipline-based professional teaching standards.

The following performance standards have been established for teachers certified to teach elementary education, English language arts, mathematics, music, physical education, science, social studies, special education and visual arts.[*]

Portfolio Score	Performance Description	Result
4	*Advanced* performance in meeting the standards	
3	*Proficient* performance in meeting the standards	Eligibility for the provisional educator certificate, provided all other requirements are met.
2	*Competent* performance in meeting the standards.	
1	*Conditional* performance in meeting the standards.	**Year 2:** Eligibility for a 3rd year in the BEST Program, additional mentoring and the submission of an additional teaching portfolio **Year 3:** Ineligibility for continued certification if standard not met by the end of the year.
Not Scorable	Incomplete or inadequate portfolio documentation which interferes with the accurate or fair scoring of the portfolio.	**Year 2:** Eligibility for a 3rd year in the BEST Program and the submission of another teaching portfolio. **Year 3:** Ineligibility for continued certification if standard not met by the end of the year.
0	Evidence of conduct in violation of the Code of Professional Responsibility for Teachers (Section 145d-400a of the certification regulations).	**Year 2:** Eligibility for a third year in the BEST Program only if requested in writing by the superintendent of schools and upon a finding of good cause by the commissioner of education. **Year 3:** Ineligibility for continued certification.

*CSDE reserves the right to implement the Completion standard instead of the Performance standard for certain categories of beginning teachers.

Section E: Portfolio Completion Standard: for all teachers serving under a Bilingual certificate or a World Languages certificate, as well as teachers of English Language Arts, Mathematics, Science or Social Studies teaching under the middle grades 4–8 (006) certification or teachers of Science and Social Studies teaching under an elementary certificate

---

In certain situations, beginning teachers are required to meet the portfolio "completion standard" instead of the "performance standard" previously described. Examples of these situations include: the pilot testing of a portfolio that has not yet been validated for teachers in a particular teaching setting, or when performance standards have not yet been finalized. For the 2003–2004 school year, this includes beginning teachers of *world languages* and those who are serving under the *bilingual* certification. In addition, the completion standard is applicable to beginning teachers who submit portfolios in English language arts, mathematics, science, or social studies while teaching under the middle grades 4–8 (006) certification, or teachers who submit portfolios in science or social studies while teaching under an elementary certificate.

The completion standard has three components: comprehensiveness, adequacy, and timeliness of submission, all of which must be met:

1. *Comprehensiveness:* All components of the teaching portfolio are present: lesson logs, videotape(s), student work, commentaries (as outlined in portfolio handbook guidelines);

2. *Adequacy:* The contents of the portfolio reflect that the beginning teacher has followed the portfolio handbook directions with regards to the period of time teaching is documented, the type of lesson and duration of lesson segments recorded on videotape, the nature and quantity of student work, and the content of the lesson commentaries (i.e., the teacher's narrative is consistent with the questions asked);

3. *Timeliness of Submission:* The portfolio must be received by the specified deadline. Exceptions to this deadline must be requested in writing to the BEST project leader for the specific subject area, and will only be granted upon finding of good cause; and

4. *Conduct in Accordance with the Code of Professional Responsibility for Professional Educators:* The teaching documented in the portfolio reflects professional and ethical conduct.

Consequences for failure to meet completion standard at the end of year two:
The beginning teacher will be required to participate for an additional year in the BEST Program and submit another portfolio during year three. A copy of the letter informing the beginning teacher that she or he has not met the completion standard will be sent to the BEST Program district facilitator and the superintendent.

Consequences for failure to meet the completion standard at the end of year three:
The beginning teacher will not have fulfilled the requirements of the BEST Program and will not be eligible for continued teaching certification. In such cases, the candidate will be eligible for reissuance of the Initial Educator Certificate only after completion of a state-approved planned program of intervening study and experience during the course of 1 school year.

Section F: Code of Professional Responsibility

All teachers licensed in the State of Connecticut are held to the Code of Professional Responsibility for Teachers (Sec. 10-145d-400a of the State Certification Regulations). All teaching documented in the portfolio must reflect professional and ethical conduct. The Teaching Portfolio Authenticity Sign-off form (see Appendix 5) must be included with all portfolios submitted for evaluation and must be signed by both the beginning teacher and the principal. Any detection of a breach of ethical conduct such as plagiarism (i.e., the taking of whole parts of portfolio exemplars or someone else's portfolio), lack of authenticity of the student work or video, or forgery (i.e., principal's signature) will be reported to the district's employing superintendent and may result in revocation of licensure.

Section G: Important Notice About Third Year Participation

Beginning teachers who submit a portfolio in year two but do not meet the portfolio standard, or beginning teachers who fail to submit a portfolio in year two have the opportunity to submit a portfolio during their third year of participation in the BEST Program. These portfolios are due **February 1,** with the final score report submitted to the beginning teacher and district by **April 1.**

*Eligibility for a Third Portfolio Submissio*n: Upon request of the superintendent of schools, third year BEST program participants who have already submitted two portfolios (one in year two and one in February of year three) and who have not yet met the acceptable performance standard *may* have one additional submission opportunity (by June 1). *This option is not available to individuals who have submitted fewer than two portfolios.*

A beginning teacher, who does not submit a portfolio or does not meet the acceptable performance standard by the end of the third year, is not eligible for a reissuance of the initial educator certificate. In such cases, the candidate will be eligible to apply for reissuance of the initial educator certificate only after completion of a state-approved planned program of intervening study and experience over the course of one school year.

Section H: Submission of Portfolio in Year One

A beginning teacher may elect to submit a portfolio in the first participation year with the approval of his or her principal and BEST district facilitator. However, research shows that beginning teachers need to focus on the development of basic teaching competencies and management of the classroom environment in the first year with the greater emphasis on content specific teaching pedagogy in year two. Therefore, it is strongly recommended that the portfolio assessment be postponed until the second year of teaching.

Analysis of Student Work: Assessment

INSTRUCTIONAL CONTEXT

The class represented in this section is AP Statistics. It consists of a class of high school seniors, ranging in age from 17 to 18 years old. This class has a broad range of abilities. There are students in my class who have never taken an AP class before and had no idea of the time, effort, or thought this class was going to require. I have students who have taken and received credit for 5 or 6 AP classes, who were very well prepared for what they were going to be required to do, and who have an interest and desire to learn AP Statistics. Of the 24 students in the class, 10 are identified as academically gifted. There is one student who is a single mother, one student with some serious health problems that require him to miss class frequently, and four students with very serious problems in their home lives. The rest of my class primarily comes from middle- to upper-class backgrounds whose parents are, for the most part, college graduates who are employed either at the local university, the hospital (we have a regional medical center and medical school), or the local pharmaceutical firm, which is our county's biggest nongovernment employer.

Since classes in statistics at the college level have such a high failure rate, many of my students enrolled in this course to get a background in

Note: Permission was given by the Nationally Board–certified teacher who wrote this reflection. (Name withheld)

statistics so they would be prepared for studying it next year. About eight of them have no plans to take the AP exam, and several who have paid deposits are unsure that they are going to. Having students with different expectations and different goals also presents an instructional challenge. Even though the students are made aware at the beginning of the year that the goal for this course is preparation for the AP exam, many take the course while not planning to take the exam and do not apply themselves as well as they should. This leads to inattentiveness in the classroom and poorly completed assignments. This has the effect of being carried over to the students who are taking the AP exam and cannot afford to be inattentive in class. It is a challenge to keep them all motivated.

There is also diversity in their educational backgrounds. I have students whose prior math courses consisted of Algebra I, Geometry, and Algebra II, and I have others who are concurrently taking AP Calculus. These differences in educational background make this class a challenge to teach. I try to balance activities that will challenge the more advanced students but at the same time not overwhelm students with less mathematical background.

PLANNING

Objectives

This assessment was taken from the unit on linear regression. The students should be able to plot a scattergram of the data, develop the least-squares regression equation, and describe, using the correlation coefficient, the strength of the relationship between the two variables. The students should be able to determine whether a significant linear relationship exists and determine, using residuals, the aptness of the linear fit. The students should also be able to demonstrate the use of confidence intervals in regression and correlation models. The students should be able to manually compute all values as well as interpret computer regression output for each of the values as it relates to the context of the problem.

Form and Content

I used a free response format for this assessment to determine the depth of student knowledge in all of the previous objectives. I did not feel that I would be able to significantly assess their knowledge if I used a multiple-choice format. The test was developed by me specifically to evaluate each of the objectives mentioned. The first problem is the regression analysis output from a statistical software program called Minitab. The students had to find the equation for the least squares line using the output (1a) and interpret the slope in the context of the problem (1b). The students then had to determine if the relationship was significant by performing a hypothesis test on the data (1c). The students had to show their understanding of confidence intervals for slope (1d), for an individual number when the price of oranges is $8 (1g), and for the average number of boxes when the price is $8 (1f). In Problem 2 the students had to show their understanding of scattergrams and graphing the line of best fit. In part c, the students also had to justify why they believed a line to be the best model for the data. In Problem 3, the students had to demonstrate their understanding of the correlation coefficient and the coefficient of determination and interpret their values. Then, in Problem 4, the students also had to demonstrate how outliers affected the slope and correlation coefficient if they were removed from the data set. Problem 2, part b, could be done either with the slope or with the correlation coefficient. If a student used the correlation coefficient, p, I gave them extra credit, as it was not part of what I taught in the unit, but the student had the option of reading about it on their own.

Mathematical Reasoning

In each of the problems, the students were asked to interpret results, define variables within the context of the situation, justify their reasoning, make conclusions, and explain their reasoning. I believe that this shows that the test was designed to elicit significant mathematical reasoning from the students. The test was not designed for students to give answers but to show that they understood and could explain what those numbers signified, not just statistically but in the context of the problem situations.

ANALYSIS OF THREE STUDENT RESPONSES

I chose three students of very different abilities and learning styles for this entry. Holly is an example of a high ability student, Amber is a student of average ability, and Kathleen is a student who tries very hard but does not always grasp the concepts completely. The three show an example of the variety of students I teach in this class and a variety of the types of responses the students give.

Holly

I chose Holly because she is an example of one of my high-achieving students. Holly studies very hard and could well be classified as an academic overachiever. She is very grade conscious and will go into a panic attack if she does not achieve an A. I believe this stems from low self-esteem on Holly's part. She is a quiet, shy, and very polite girl. She is also very overweight. Holly presents an instructional challenge in her reaction to her grades. As an instructor who cares about her students, it is very difficult for me to watch Holly break down and leave my room in tears in reaction to a grade. It tends to make me feel guilty, and I have to guard myself to grade her tests fairly and with the same standards as the other students. She is never upset with me, just herself, but as a teacher, I feel responsible. It rarely happens that her tests are less than adequate for her standards because she works hard to make sure she does well.

Content Mastery

I believe that Holly's test shows that she mastered the concepts of the unit. Three of the five mistakes she made (1c, d, and h) were due to errors in simple arithmetic or, in the case of Problem 1, part h, looking up the value in the row above the one she needed. Her other two mistakes were more critical. In Problem 1, part e, Holly confused the coefficient of determination, r^2, with the correlation coefficient, r. This is a very easy mistake to make for 1st-year statistics students, and I believe Holly will not make that same mistake again. In Problem 4, however, Holly showed that she might have some misconceptions about the correlation coefficient or at least why it will change when the outlier is removed.

Mathematical Reasoning

Throughout Holly's paper, she shows mathematical thinking and reasoning in response to each question. In Problem 1, she shows her understanding of the slope of the least squares line in part b and clearly states her conclusion in part c. In Problem 2, she justifies why she feels that a line is a good model for the data through her use of residuals. In Problem 4, Holly again correctly interprets the slope in the context of the problem and explains how the slope of the line will change if the outlier is removed from the data in part d. Because she can explain and justify and not just find answers, I believe this shows Holly's understanding of the procedures she is performing. The procedures are not the end in themselves but what they mean in the context of each problem. Holly shows that reasoning throughout her paper.

Feedback

I go over each problem in class when I hand back the test. Holly asked questions about what she got wrong and was able to understand and correct her mistakes. I also told her specifically to practice her arithmetic because even though she understood the concepts clearly she also needs to be able to get the correct answer. I told her that if she were working for a corporation and not just taking statistics as a class, her research and her job would depend on accuracy.

Amber

I chose Amber because she exemplifies my "average" student. Amber is bright but does not study any harder than she has to. She is very pretty and very popular and also a talented athlete. For these reasons, she tends to put studying third on her list of priorities, after sports and socializing. As a learner, Amber tends to be a "cookbook" learner. She wants to have a recipe for doing each problem that she can follow every time, having to put in little thought of her own. Because of this, Amber's answers can be very canned. She always wants to know when I am teaching a subject, how I would state my conclusion, or justify a response. Her response to a similar prompt on a test will be exactly like I phrased it. It is a challenge for me to get Amber to think on her own and to take risks in her ideas.

In Problem 1, Amber showed some misconceptions in parts g and h in her interpretation of the Minitab printout. She also was careless in her definition of the slope in part b and did not consider what the values represented. This mistake was very significant because if she had just read what she wrote, I would like to think she would have realized that it was very unrealistic. This shows Amber's reluctance to take a risk; she is more worried about how she is saying it than what she is saying. Amber also shows a gap in her prior knowledge in Problem 2, in plotting the least squares line. Plotting lines is a topic that I reviewed but is initially taught in Algebra I. Amber also had not mastered the concept of residuals, as indicated by the blank answer on her paper. In her answer to Problem 3 (on notebook paper), she does show that she mastered the concept of r and r^2 and hypothesis testing for significant correlation between variables. Problem 4 indicates Amber's misconception about the slope in parts b and c, and she does not read the problem carefully or fully answer it.

Mathematical Reasoning

Amber shows that she is capable of doing the computations. Mathematically, her arithmetic is correct. Her reasoning however, is flawed. Her conclusion to Problem 1, part b, is wrong even though her understanding of the printout is correct. She rejects the null hypothesis but then concludes that she does not have enough evidence to prove her alternative, which she does. She shows significant understanding of r and r^2 with her interpretation to each in Problem 3. The flawed reasoning that most concerns me is her interpretations of the slope in Problems 1 and 4. She understands what is happening; she just has her variables turned around. But she should have realized that by her illogical answers. Neither one makes sense. In Problem 1, part b, she states, "For every box (of oranges sold) there is a $763 increase in price." In Problem 4, she states, ".0534 is the number of the students enrolled in grades 9–12 for every state." She understood what numbers went in the sentence but displayed no understanding of what they meant or where they went. If she had taken the time to read the sentence, she might have realized her mistake.

Feedback

Amber needed remediation in three areas: understanding and interpreting the slope, graphing lines, and using residuals to justify the linear model. I met with Amber and several other students who needed help with these concepts before school for a few days (as I do cover all tests for students who need extra help). I also keep encouraging Amber to use her own words so she would have better understanding of the material. I also started doing more group projects with this class. I thought Amber and several other students who have the same problem would benefit from working with other students and trying to explain and justify their conclusions to them.

Kathleen

Kathleen is a hard worker but tends to be a low-functioning student. I chose her as a representative of the students in my class who struggle with the difficult concepts in statistics. Kathleen regularly comes by for extra help after school; does, or at least attempts, all her homework; and still does not make the grades she would like. She signed up for statistics because all her friends were in the class. Kathleen is the type of student who pays attention in class, and while you are going over the material and discussing it, she can answer any question you ask her. Once she leaves class, she forgets everything she knows. When she comes by for help after school, I reteach the lesson again. She might retain 40% of what we have done the second time. I go over homework in class the next day and, essentially, as I am doing the problems, go over the concepts again. By the time the unit test comes, Kathleen has had more hours of instruction than anyone in the class and probably studied harder; however, her grade will be one of the lowest in the class. Because of this, Kathleen can be a challenge to teach. I have encouraged her to use a tape recorder to help at night while she is doing her homework, but she refuses.

Content Mastery

Kathleen has missed some essential concepts of the unit. Based on her response to Problems 1 and 4, it is apparent that she does not know how to read a computer printout for the information it contains. She could not find the least squares line, define the slope, find the coefficient of determination, or compute the confidence intervals when asked in Problem 1. In Problem 4, similarly, she had no understanding of how the values in parts c and d would change if the outlier was removed from them. She also has some gaps in her knowledge hypothesis testing. She understood the majority of the setup of the test in Problem 1, part c, but in Problem 3, part b, when asked to do the same type of problem, she did not know how to start but wrote down numbers. This kind of inconsistency is typical of Kathleen.

Mathematical Reasoning

Kathleen's mathematical reasoning can be seen in three places. The first place is Problem 1, part c. In this problem, even though she uses the wrong number to calculate her t value, she does understand what the t value means in terms of her problem and states the correct conclusion based on her answer. I also think that Problem 3, part a, shows her understanding of what r and r^2 mean. Even though she doesn't correctly calculate r^2, she does understand that it represents the variation in the problem. If r^2 was incorrect, then r also was incorrect, but she does show that she understands that the values are positively correlated. However, she missed the important fact that r should always be values of −1 and 1. Kathleen shows incorrect reasoning in her conclusion to part c of Problem 3 because she bases the relationship of the line on the residuals and completely forgets about the information she had drawn in the previous part. The blank responses on her test show her inability to make connections and reason through the problems, with or without the practical knowledge of being able to calculate the correct number.

Feedback

Kathleen and I covered every problem on her test again after school. We went over mistakes in concepts and discussed how she could improve her score by at least expanding on what things meant, even if she could not get the correct numerical answer. I give her credit for what is right in the response so that even if she got the wrong value she could have partial credit for her explanations and justifications.

Reflection

Further Instruction

After evaluating my students' performance on this test, I felt confident about their understanding of the important concepts of this unit. I learned that, for the most part, they were capable of performing the correct calculations or interpretations of computer-generated data for the objectives stated previously for this unit. Furthermore, they showed significant mathematical reasoning in their justifications, conclusions, and interpretations of those results.

Holly's paper suggests that she is ready to move on to the next concept. Her mistakes are simple arithmetic, which is mainly due to carelessness, not a lack of understanding of the concepts. My evidence for this is her responses both in performing the mathematical calculations and in her justifications and the conclusions she states. Holly has learned the material presented and has displayed that knowledge with confidence, evidenced in all her responses.

Amber's paper suggests that she is also ready to move on to the next concept. Though she does not display the depth of understanding that Holly exhibits, she still clearly has mastered the majority of the concepts. I think Amber needs to spend some time before or after school reviewing some of the concepts that she had difficulty with, such as the meaning of the slope and understanding of residual. Amber and I, along with a few more of her classmates that needed the same type of help, did spend some time before school in remediation.

Kathleen's paper suggests more of a challenge. The majority of my class is ready to move on to the next concept, but Kathleen is not. Since Kathleen has been attending regular sessions with me after school, I decided that the best course for her was to remediate the concepts she missed during these one-on-one sessions. The evidence for her lack of understanding of the basic concepts can be seen in the many blank spaces on her test, where she really had no understanding of how to attempt the problem.

Evaluation of Assessment

I thought the test was a good overall picture of the concepts the students should know. It addressed each objective in a clear and precise manner. It allowed me to assess the students' ability to perform the basic calculations through the computational part of each problem. It also allowed me to evaluate their understanding of what these answers represent through their responses to the conclusion or justification part to each problem.

If I use this assessment again, I might try adding some multiple choice problems to give the students a variety of testing formats. I also need to fix the typographical errors in Problem 1, where I have *fives* in the first line instead of *gives*, and I left out part f in labeling the parts to the problem.

A FEW THOUGHTS ABOUT THE COMMENTARY

The commentary follows the basic process of reflection presented in Chapter 3: description, analysis, and future impact. Specific questions asked in the activity are answered. The reflection is well written and is within the page limit required by the NBPTS. This candidate has done an excellent job with this commentary. If there are still questions about reflection, Chapter 3 should be reread.

Council for Exceptional Children Standards

The Council for Exceptional Children is the leading professional organization for teachers of children with special needs. This organization has developed professional practice standards. These can be used as a framework for developing a professional portfolio.

THE STANDARDS

The standards are divided into five areas: (1) Instructional Responsibilities, (2) Management of Behavior, (3) Support Procedures, (4) Parent Relationships, and (5) Advocacy. Each section has quality indicators that describe and give definition to the area. For example, the area of Instructional Responsibilities is outlined below. For quality indicators in all five areas, refer to www.cec.sped.org.

Area: Instructional Responsibilities

Special education personnel are committed to the application of professional expertise to ensure the provision of quality education for all individuals with exceptionalities. Professionals strive to:

1. Identify and use instructional methods and curricula that are appropriate to their area of professional practice and effective in meeting the individual needs of persons with exceptionalities.
2. Participate in the selection and use of appropriate instructional materials, equipment, supplies, and other resources needed in the effective practice of their profession.
3. Create safe and effective learning environments, which contribute to the fulfillment of needs, stimulation of learning, and self-concept.
4. Maintain class size and case loads that are conducive to meeting the individual needs of individuals with exceptionalities.
5. Use assessment instruments and procedures that do not discriminate against persons with exceptionalities on the basis of race, color, creed, sex, national origin, age, political practices, family or social background, sexual orientation, or exceptionality.
6. Base grading, promotion, graduation, and movement out of the program on the individual goals and objectives for individuals with exceptionalities.
7. Provide accurate program data to administrators, colleagues, and parents, based on efficient and objective record-keeping practices, for the purpose of decision making.
8. Maintain confidentiality of information except when information is released under specific conditions of written consent and statutory confidentiality requirements.

HOW CAN A PORTFOLIO BE ORGANIZED AROUND THESE STANDARDS?

A portfolio would be organized much like the INTASC examples presented in Chapter 2 or Chapter 6, depending on its purpose. A product or showcase portfolio would be appropriate to develop for these standards.

For a product design, the portfolio could easily be divided into the five areas. Evidence would be placed in each of the areas to support the quality indicators. One reflection could be written per area.

These standards could also be used as a teacher recruitment tool or as an alternative evaluation model. A showcase portfolio could be developed around the five areas for job interviews, including evidence that demonstrates the indicators. Alternative evaluation portfolio developers could use the professional goal framework, choosing an area (or two) as their professional goals. Evidence would document how the goal (area) was being met. This model would be particularly effective as a precursor to the National Board process.

Canadian Curriculum Standards: Foundation Statements for Science Literacy

Canada is mirroring the United States by creating sets of national standards for various curriculum areas. These standards are being developed across the provinces. One of the first areas developed was science literacy. The science literacy standards are based on four foundational statements:

1. Students will develop an understanding of the nature of science and technology, of the relationship between science and technology, and of the social and environmental contexts of science and technology.
2. Students will develop the skills required for scientific and technological inquiry, for solving problems, for communicating scientific ideas and results, for working collaboratively, and for making informed decisions.
3. Students will construct knowledge and understandings of concepts in life science, physical science, and Earth and space science, and apply these understandings.

4. Students will be encouraged to develop attitudes that support the responsible acquisition and application of scientific and technological knowledge to the mutual benefit of self, society, and the environment.

HOW CAN A PORTFOLIO BE ORGANIZED AROUND THESE STANDARDS?

If a teacher wanted to show that these standards were being met, a product portfolio could be developed, with each foundational belief becoming an area or domain. Student work related to learning outcomes would be included. Reflections could focus on how the teacher is meeting the foundational standards.

National Council for Teachers of Mathematics K–12 Standards

The National Council for Teachers of Mathematics was one of the first professional groups to create a set of national standards related to student learning. These 10 standards are divided into two areas: (1) mathematical content students should learn and (2) mathematical processes through which students should acquire and use their mathematical knowledge.

THE STANDARDS

Mathematical content standards include:

1. Number and Operations
2. Patterns, Functions, and Algebra
3. Geometry and Spatial Sense
4. Measurement
5. Data Analysis, Statistics, and Probability

Mathematical processes:

1. Problem solving
2. Reasoning and proof
3. Communication
4. Connections
5. Representation

For each standard, quality indicators are given. For example, Standard 1—Number and Operations:

Mathematics instructional programs should foster the development of number and operation sense so that all students:

- Understand numbers, ways of representing numbers, relationships among numbers, and number systems
- Understand the meaning of operations and how they relate to each other
- Use computational tools and strategies fluently and estimate appropriately

HOW CAN A PORTFOLIO BE ORGANIZED AROUND THESE STANDARDS?

A product portfolio could be developed around the two areas—content and processes. Developers would include evidence for each of the standards (five for each area) recognizing each quality indicator. One might think it would be easier to show standards individually, but this can be difficult, especially since the standards overlap. By dividing the portfolio into two broad areas, content and processes, more flexibility is given to the developer. Reflections can be written for each of the two areas.

NUMBER AND OPERATIONS STANDARD*

Instructional programs from prekindergarten through Grade 12 should enable all students to do the following:

Understand Numbers, Ways of Representing Numbers, Relationships Among Numbers, and Number Systems

Pre-K–2 Expectations

In prekindergarten through Grade 2, all students should:

- Count with understanding and recognize "how many" in sets of objects.
- Use multiple models to develop initial understanding of place value and the base 10 number system.

- Develop understanding of the relative position and magnitude of whole numbers and of ordinal and cardinal numbers and their connections.
- Develop a sense of whole numbers and represent and use them in flexible ways, including relating, composing, and decomposing numbers.
- Connect number words and numerals to the quantities they represent, using various physical models and representations.
- Understand and represent commonly used fractions, such as 1/4, 1/3, and 1/2.

Grades 3–5 Expectations

In Grades 3–5 all students should:

- Understand the place-value structure of the base 10 number system and be able to represent and compare whole numbers and decimals.
- Recognize equivalent representations for the same number and generate them by decomposing and composing numbers.
- Develop understanding of fractions as parts of unit wholes, as parts of a collection, as locations on number lines, and as divisions of whole numbers.
- Use models, benchmarks, and equivalent forms to judge the size of fractions.
- Recognize and generate equivalent forms of commonly used fractions, decimals, and percents.
- Explore numbers less than 0 by extending the number line and using familiar applications.
- Describe classes of numbers according to characteristics such as the nature of their factors.

Grades 6–8 Expectations

In Grades 6–8 all students should:

- Work flexibly with fractions, decimals, and percents to solve problems.
- Compare and order fractions, decimals, and percents efficiently and find their approximate locations on a number line.
- Develop meaning for percents greater than 100 and less than 1.
- Understand and use ratios and proportions to represent quantitative relationships.
- Develop an understanding of large numbers and recognize and appropriately use exponential, scientific, and calculator notation.
- Use factors, multiples, prime factorization, and relatively prime numbers to solve problems.
- Develop meaning for integers and represent and compare quantities with them.

Grades 9–12 Expectations

In Grades 9–12 all students should:

- Develop a deeper understanding of very large and very small numbers and of various representations of them.

- Compare and contrast the properties of numbers and number systems, including the rational and real numbers, and understand complex numbers as solutions to quadratic equations that do not have real solutions.
- Understand vectors and matrices as systems that have some of the properties of the real-number system.
- Use number theory arguments to justify relationships involving whole numbers.

Understand Meanings of Operations and How They Relate to One Another

Pre-K–2 Expectations

In prekindergarten through Grade 2 all students should:

- Understand various meanings of addition and subtraction of whole numbers and the relationship between the two operations.
- Understand the effects of adding and subtracting whole numbers.
- Understand situations that entail multiplication and division, such as equal groupings of objects and sharing equally.

Grades 3–5 Expectations

In Grades 3–5 all students should:

- Understand various meanings of multiplication and division.
- Understand the effects of multiplying and dividing whole numbers.
- Identify and use relationships between operations, such as division as the inverse of multiplication, to solve problems.
- Understand and use properties of operations, such as the distributivity of multiplication over addition.

Grades 6–8 Expectations

In Grades 6–8 all students should:

- Understand the meaning and effects of arithmetic operations with fractions, decimals, and integers.
- Use the associative and commutative properties of addition and multiplication and the distributive property of multiplication over addition to simplify computations with integers, fractions, and decimals.
- Understand and use the inverse relationships of addition and subtraction, multiplication and division, and squaring and finding square roots to simplify computations and solve problems.

Grades 9–12 Expectations

In Grades 9–12 all students should:

- Judge the effects of such operations as multiplication, division, and computing powers and roots on the magnitudes of quantities.

- Develop an understanding of properties of, and representations for, the addition and multiplication of vectors and matrices.
- Develop an understanding of permutations and combinations as counting techniques.

Compute Fluently and Make Reasonable Estimates

Pre-K–2 Expectations

In prekindergarten through Grade 2 all students should:

- Develop and use strategies for whole-number computations, with a focus on addition and subtraction.
- Develop fluency with basic number combinations for addition and subtraction.
- Use a variety of methods and tools to compute, including objects, mental computation, estimation, paper and pencil, and calculators.

Grades 3–5 Expectations

In Grades 3–5 all students should:

- Develop fluency with basic number combinations for multiplication and division and use these combinations to mentally compute related problems, such as 30×50.
- Develop fluency in adding, subtracting, multiplying, and dividing whole numbers.
- Develop and use strategies to estimate the results of whole-number computations and to judge the reasonableness of such results.
- Develop and use strategies to estimate computations involving fractions and decimals in situations relevant to students' experience.
- Use visual models, benchmarks, and equivalent forms to add and subtract commonly used fractions and decimals.
- Select appropriate methods and tools for computing with whole numbers from among mental computation, estimation, calculators, and paper and pencil according to the context and nature of the computation and use the selected method or tools.

Grades 6–8 Expectations

In Grades 6–8 all students should:

- Select appropriate methods and tools for computing with fractions and decimals from among mental computation, estimation, calculators or computers, and paper and pencil, depending on the situation, and apply the selected methods.
- Develop and analyze algorithms for computing with fractions, decimals, and integers and develop fluency in their use.
- Develop and use strategies to estimate the results of rational-number computations and judge the reasonableness of the results.

- Develop, analyze, and explain methods for solving problems involving proportions, such as scaling and finding equivalent ratios.

Grades 9–12 Expectations

In Grades 9–12 all students should:

- Develop fluency in operations with real numbers, vectors, and matrices, using mental computation or paper-and-pencil calculations for simple cases and technology for more-complicated cases.
- Judge the reasonableness of numerical computations and their results.

International Society for Technology in Education's National Educational Technology Standards (NETS) and Performance Indicators for Teachers

All classroom teachers should be prepared to meet the following standards and performance indicators:

I. Technology Operations and Concepts
    Teachers demonstrate a sound understanding of technology operations and concepts. Teachers:

    A. Demonstrate introductory knowledge, skills, and understanding of concepts related to technology (as described in the ISTE *National Educational Technology Standards for Students*).
    B. Demonstrate continual growth in technology knowledge and skills to stay abreast of current and emerging technologies.

II. Planning and Designing Learning Environments and Experiences
Teachers plan and design effective learning environments and experiences supported by technology. Teachers:

   A. Design developmentally appropriate learning opportunities that apply technology-enhanced instructional strategies to support the diverse needs of learners.
   B. Apply current research on teaching and learning with technology when planning learning environments and experiences.
   C. Identify and locate technology resources and evaluate them for accuracy and suitability.
   D. Plan for the management of technology resources within the context of learning activities.
   E. Plan strategies to manage student learning in a technology-enhanced environment.

III. Teaching, Learning, and the Curriculum
Teachers implement curriculum plans that include methods and strategies for applying technology to maximize student learning. Teachers:

   A. Facilitate technology-enhanced experiences that address content standards and student technology standards.
   B. Use technology to support learner-centered strategies that address the diverse needs of students.
   C. Apply technology to develop students' higher order skills and creativity.
   D. Manage student learning activities in a technology-enhanced environment.

IV. Assessment and Evaluation
Teachers apply technology to facilitate a variety of effective assessment and evaluation strategies. Teachers:

   A. Apply technology in assessing student learning of subject matter using a variety of assessment techniques.
   B. Use technological resources to collect and analyze data, interpret results, and communicate findings to improve instructional practice and maximize student learning.
   C. Apply multiple methods of evaluation to determine students' appropriate use of technology resources for learning, communication, and productivity.

V. Productivity and Professional Practice
Teachers use technology to enhance their productivity and professional practice. Teachers:

   A. Use technology resources to engage in ongoing professional development and lifelong learning.

B. Continually evaluate and reflect on professional practice to make informed decisions regarding the use of technology in support of student learning.
C. Apply technology to increase productivity.
D. Use technology to communicate and collaborate with peers, parents, and the larger community to nurture student learning.

VI. Social, Ethical, Legal, and Human Issues

Teachers understand the social, ethical, legal, and human issues surrounding the use of technology in PK–12 schools and apply that understanding in practice. Teachers:

A. Model and teach legal and ethical practice related to the use of technology.
B. Apply technology to enable and empower learners with diverse backgrounds, characteristics, and abilities.
C. Identify and use technology that affirms diversity.
D. Promotes safe and healthy use of technology.
E. Facilitate equitable access to technology for all students.

INDEX